To Jimmy Kirkpatrick, newspaperman
and state official Supreme, with
appreciation for your friendship and
your many kindnesses to our newspaper
carrier boys and girls of the State of Missouri.

Sincerely, Frances

ED WATSON - COUNTRY EDITOR

His Life and Times

Edwin Moss Watson, Editor and Proprietor of the *Columbia Daily Tribune* from 1905 until 1937. Portrait painted by Ned Etheridge, a son of Watson's good friend, W.C. Etheridge.

ED WATSON - COUNTRY EDITOR

His Life and Times

Leslie Francis Pike

Bachelor of Journalism
University of Missouri

Contents

Today's Business

Politics

Sports

Boosting a Town

Lynching

Friends

Three Score and Ten

Notes

Edwin Moss Chronology

Tribune Chronology

Acknowledgments

Index of Names

Illustrations

Foreword

To all newspaper men and women—past, present and future—who are not "Journalists," especially those who have made comments on this book and have put up with my shortcomings—with no apologies whatsoever for having scooped them on this book. This biography has as much right to be written as all those books that display the talents and foibles of William Allen White, contemporary of Ed Watson.

To the University of Missouri's Walter Williams for the inspiration he gave me in my first journalism class—the History and Principles of Journalism, and for the tears he shed when he gave his last lecture in H.&P., before he moved over to the President's house, several hundred feet south of the journalism school he founded in 1908.

To William Hirth for giving me my first job—on the *Missouri Farmer,* and for calling Ed Watson to get me my second and final job—on the *Tribune.* But most of all, to my grandfather, Jerome F. Green of Rush Hill, Mo., for paying Hirth's first year's expenses at M.U., and for giving me a note of introduction to Bill Hirth.

Richelieu once boasted: "If you give me six lines written by the hand of the most honest man, I will find something in them with which to hang him." To those of you who excel in the art of criticism, have fun. I am sure this will give you grist for your mill, so hack and grind away.

I have avoided, with a superior air, the psychoanalytic approach, which is the habit of modern biographers. An individual can never explain himself, but many writers, even with a superficial knowledge of others, frequently take it upon themselves to describe in detail the innermost thoughts of their subjects about whom they know little.

Beginnings

Circus at Millersburg

The circus came to town. Then came the rains. There were clowns, jugglers, acrobats, magicians, animals and animal trainers. There were tents and huge tent poles, wagons and horses. The rain and mud prevented erection of the "Big Top," and because of the muddy roads, the circus people were stranded in Millersburg, Callaway County, Missouri. Performers visited the homes of villagers, including that of Dr. B.A. Watson. Each night there were impromptu performances all over town. The year was 1872, and little Edwin Moss Watson, four-year-old son of Dr. and Mrs. Watson, was in "seventh heaven."

Years later, Watson related the story of the circus that was forced to stay over in Millersburg as his earliest and most memorable recollection. Those were joyful evenings when clowns performed their outlandish tricks, jugglers did the impossible and magicians mystified. Edwin was delighted, as were the other children of Millersburg.

Ed Watson's interest in circus people continued long after he became nationally famous as "Editor and Proprietor" of a country newspaper, *The Columbia Daily Tribune.* Advance men, those who promoted the circus ahead of its visit to a town, were always welcomed by Ed Watson. His was a familiar name in the circus and show business world. In exchange for advertising in the Tribune, passes to the circus were issued to Col. Watson* who gave them, not only to Tribune staffers and friends, but especially to the carrier and street sales boys.

Edwin Moss Watson was born in Millersburg November 29, 1867, to Dr. Berry Allen Watson and Clara (Ward) Watson. He was the second of six children, the oldest, Estelle "Stella," born

1

in Williamsburg, Mo., Edwin, Margaret and Mattie in Millersburg and the youngest two, Laws and Carson, in Columbia.

A 4-Yr-Old Moves to Columbia

Shortly after the circus loaded its wagons and moved out of Millersburg, young Edwin and his parents also moved out, going to Columbia. His father located a place for the family to live, and then looked around for a school for his two oldest children, Stella and Edwin. Mission School* built by pioneer merchant, J.L. Stephens, was taking young boys and girls at the age of five, and the Watson children were duly enrolled.

Thus began the education and distinguished career of young Edwin. For the intermediate grades he attended the Baptist Female Academy, now Stephens College. His undergraduate days at the hometown University of Missouri earned him the A.B. degree and a Phi Beta Kappa key. Following several years work on out-of-town newspapers, he returned to Columbia to enter law school, and in 1897 received his LL.B. degree, magna cum laude.

Woodson Plantation Home

After five years in Columbia, Dr. Watson decided to purchase a home. An opportunity arose to buy a large home at the southern edge of Columbia, directly east of what is now the University of Missouri School of Journalism. It was the old Woodson place and one of the first homes built in the area. Judge Warren Woodson started building it in 1819, and established it as the homesite for the large Woodson plantation. Columbia did not exist. But a mile northwest of the Woodson plantation was the town of Smithton, situated on a hill above free-flowing, spring-fed Flat Branch.*

Judge Woodson had many slaves who built and lived in a row of "slave cabins" at the rear of the plantation home. Later,

Dr. Berry Allen Watson, father of Edwin Moss Watson. Dr. Watson was a physician with a general practice in the Columbia area from 1872 until his death January 19, 1918. One of Dr. Watson's foxhounds also shown in picture.

Clara Ward Watson, mother of Edwin Moss Watson, in her new home at 8 Watson Place. This is the picture that was used in 1919 in her book of poems, "My Yesterdays."

the cabins were used by the Watsons as sleeping rooms for a dozen or more students attending the university. Inside the commodious plantation home were more rooms for students and a big dining room where boarders were attended by the Watson servants,* presided over by Clara Watson.

Home Away From Home

For many years the Watson place was a home-away-from-home for many university men. At the time, there were no dormitories on the campus and many Columbians opened their doors to students. The two-story home was located on a hill facing west, just south of Elm Street. Sixteen limestone steps started from street level up to the walk that led to the front porch. The house had a well, but many of the occupants filled their jugs with water from across Ninth Street at the old spring house.* It was supposed at the time that the water had medicinal properties, and all availed themselves of the water that flowed at a good rate from the spring. In that day there were many springs all over the downtown of Columbia and each time a basement was dug for a new building, springs were a problem.

The original structure of the old Woodson home was a double-log house built after the fashion of pioneer days with a roofed porch between two large rooms called a dog-trot. The logs were hewn from mammoth oak trees. Afterwards the one-story log house was increased to two stories, and still later an L was added. With the addition of "the cottage," a three-story building, the number of rooms was increased to thirteen. Judge Woodson also built "the cabin," a two-story building of four rooms, and it was occupied for many years by servants of both post-bellum and ante-bellum days.

All weatherboarding on the house, the doors to most rooms, including the doors to the huge living room, and the inside woodwork were cut from large walnut trees that grew in

3

profusion on a piece of land that reached from present-day Ninth Street to what is now College Avenue. The mantels in the house were carved walnut, artistically designed.

Inside the home, Ed listed a few items common to the late 1800's. Shells and pebbles loaded a corner what-not. Across the room a pink glass vase filled with cat-tails occupied another corner. An enlarged picture of a grandparent in a corrugated frame sat on a side table, as did the family album bound in yellow plush containing pictures of Aunt Polly's beaux. A conch shell held the dining room door back. In front of an easy chair, rested a footstool made of tin cans and covered with whip-stitched felt. Curtain cord tidies graced the back of a rocking chair, and on the front stoop a door mat greeted all visitors and guests with WELCOME in large letters.

Born at the home in 1827 was a daughter, Susan Woodson, who at the age of eighteen years, married James Moss. They were the parents of Mrs. E.W. Stephens, whose husband directed young Edwin's interest in the newspaper business.

The old place was known many years as "Fort Woodson" to hundreds of men all over Missouri and throughout the nation who made their home in this historic place during their student days at the University. Many of these men became prominent in various parts of the country.

The home had been abandoned for several years prior to its razing in 1914. During those years it became an object of curiosity. Ed wrote that "many mysterious and romantic stories were circulated regarding it." The one most credited was the belief that the old house was haunted. Stories of "nocturnal visits of phantom shapes that swept through the old halls and lingered around the scenes of their earthly abode 'till the cock's shrill clarion note, warned them of the approach of day," were rife; and watchers might often be seen in the moonlight, "peering through the casements of the old house, fearful but hopeful of surprising these walkers of the night."

"In a few days," Watson continued, "the ground where this

4

old landmark has stood for nearly a century will be bare, and one more relic of Columbia's past will be but a memory."

Dogs and Horses

Dogs and horses were an important part of Watson's youth. His education was classical, and later writings would draw deeply upon his extensive readings in Latin and Greek. Dogs and horses also played a part in his adult life. He never learned to drive an automobile. He was a harness racing judge at the Missouri State Fair for a number of years. His admiration for horses was inherited from his father, who not only was an excellent judge of horseflesh, but one who owned several fine saddlers. Dr. Watson did not train his horses for the ring. But he was a splendid and graceful rider himself, and found pleasure in showing his horses to his friends. He was especially fond of running-walk horses that could cover much ground in a hurry and with ease. On calls to his patients, horseback was his mode of travel.

* * *

Dr. B.A. Watson

Berry Allen Watson was born in Charlotte County, Virginia, in 1833, and came with his parents to Callaway County, Missouri, at the age of six. He graduated from Westminster College, Fulton, in 1857. In 1860, he taught school in Lafayette County, where he joined Capt. Joseph Shelby and his Confederate Army as the War Between the States broke out. He entered Louisville Medical College, Kentucky, in 1863 and on May 4, 1864, married Clara Ward of Callaway County. He then entered Belleview Medical College, New York, where he graduated in 1866. Following graduation he entered the practice of medicine at Williamsburg, Mo.

Clara Ward Watson

Dr. Watson's bride of more than a half-century, was born at the old Hunt place near Cedar Creek on September 18, 1842, the daughter of John Milton and Margaret (Hunt) Ward, and the granddaughter of Dr. and Mrs. John Wilson Ward. Dr. Ward was the first graduate physician to practice in Callaway County. Both families were pioneer residents of Callaway, coming to that county from Kentucky.

Clara attended Christian College at the age of ten in 1852, the first year the institution gave instruction. Later, she enrolled in Baptist College, now Stephens College. But when President . J.A. Hollis left the college at Columbia to accept the presidency of Baptist College at Lexington, Missouri, Clara transferred to Lexington, and later graduated. Upon graduation she cast lots with a close girl-friend for the Valedictory. But her friend won the top honors and Clara was awarded the Salutatory.

Clara Watson possessed no little literary ability. Letters to her children were often couched in verse that told of the incidents and happenings in home and town. This talent, because of her native modesty, was known but to few. She was the author of a little volume of verse "My Yesterdays," gotten together with the encouragement of Edwin, and appropriately illustrated by Cousin James H. Moss. In verse, she tells of childhood recollections and impressions of later years. A hundred volumes were printed and presented to friends.

The Hunt Home on Cedar Creek

Although the Watson family had lived in Boone County since 1872, the family considered the old Hunt plantation as home. It is located about two and one-half miles southwest of Millersburg near Cedar Creek. The acreage was first entered at the Franklin Land Office in 1825 by Wilson Hunt, Clara's grandfather. It consisted of 1,280 acres. Much of the land was in creek bottom and most of it in timber. The early settlers looked for two things when searching for a new home—timber and water. Both

The old Woodson Plantation Home, South Ninth and Elm
streets, bought by Dr. Watson in 1876. In 1918 Clara Ward Watson wrote: "When Judge Warren Woodson bought the land
near a hundred years ago, it was thickly timbered and considered quite out of town. There was no thought of having the
State University in the woodland just opposite...it was here we
reared our children...the old house has passed away, but there
are many who have been inmates of the 'Old Manse' who will
cherish the happy associations which cluster around it as a sweet
memory."

Woodson(Watson) Home on South Ninth Street as it was in
1915. A more complete view is shown below.

The Hunt Home, built by Wilson and Edy (Ingle) Hunt on a hill over-looking Cedar Creek near Millersburg. It is still standing. Clara Ward Watson wrote: "My grandfather Hunt moved from Kentucky to Missouri early in the eighteenth century, settling in Callaway County. He built the first brick house in the county. My grandparents were noted for their hospitality and benevolence; their home was 'la refuge' for many a weary one who would come seeking a home and some would say—'a place to die.' In the family grave yard there are more graves of those not related, than of the family." Clara's brother, John Wilson Ward Sr., is to her right in the picture and on her left is her son, Edwin Moss Watson.

were plentiful on the Hunt plantation.

Wilson Hunt brought his slaves with him from Kentucky and shortly after arriving he built the first brick home in Callaway County. The style of architecture is what is known today as Federal. Among Hunt's slaves were master artisans and the bricks for the story and a half building were burned by these artisans east of the housesite. Small mounds stand today where the bricks were hand-made.

Clara was born there, and spent her girlhood in the home that remained in the family more than a century. As a child, Edwin spent many happy hours roaming the woods and creeks, and delighted in taking some of his young friends on cave-exploring expeditions near the creek.

The Hunt place was the gathering place for all the Wards and Watsons. Many of the holidays were spent there, and on several July 4th holidays, Edwin brought out fireworks, putting some excitement into the lives of the Ward and Watson children. Edwin knew that his mother was fond of her birthplace and he made it a point to see that the family grave site was carefully tended, that the fence around it was in good repair, that the grounds were kept clean and that the tombstones were upright. This became Ed's project, following the death of his father in 1918. He and his mother visited the family plot and, although his father was buried in Columbia Cemetery, there were others in the family that his mother wanted to keep alive in her memory. Ed's visits to the cemetery continued past his mother's death in 1927. She was buried beside her husband in Columbia Cemetery, but Ed continued to care for the old cemetery at the Hunt place, possibly because he knew his mother would want him to do it.

Boarding House Habitue'

Mention has been made of the boarders taken in by the Watson family. Ed Watson was a customer at boarding houses most of his life. At the South Ninth Street home he knew the life of a boarder from the time he was nine years old.

The influence of a boarding house, and also the influence that Texas had on his life, was demonstrated shortly after he bought the *Tribune.* He started a column that he called "MAV-ERICKS," and his explanation for the name follows:

Mavericks, in the parlance of the big cattle ranchers of the west, are the stray unbranded animals, corralled and branded by the finder at the roundup. That is what the thoughts in this column are—stray quips and notions that cannot be classed as editorial or news, yet which seem interesting enough to be "corralled." They are the chips that fly from the making of the rest of the paper, and though stray, they are all from the Tribune's own ranges. They are not written with the scissors.

In the same issue he wrote:

What I dislike about a boarding house is that your little share of eternity is broken into bits by requests to please be on time for your meals. Now I delight not to be on time for meals. It shows, my superiority to mere circumstances to violate the temporal regularity of the cuisine; to come an hour late and have dinner served in that state of savoury warmth, or chill that it would have had an hour before. This is being master of one's Fate.

Five days later he found a Texas item about a boarding housekeeper who was besieged by the police because she had her provisions sent to her through the mails. Ed's Maverick comment was:

The size of a piece of steak you get sometimes in Missouri might seem to indicate that it had been sent by wireless telegraphy.

Among the boarders at the Watson place were young Jimmy Garth and his mother. Mrs. Garth's husband, James Garth Sr., died when their son, Jimmy, was six months old. Later when Jimmy was six years old, his mother moved with him into the Watson home. This was an exciting place for young Jimmy and he had many pleasant memories of his stay at the big house on South Ninth Street.

"I recall with a special fondness," said Garth, "that Ed, who was in law school, came down the steps from his upstairs bedroom to breakfast each morning, greeting me with 'How's your copperosity?' I never found the meaning of the expression but I appreciated the recognition."

"Carson was the youngest of the Watson family of six," Garth continued. "Mattie had died at the age of ten some years before and so there were five children remaining, all young men and women, except Carson, who was about seven years older than I."

"Carson and his gang of young hoodlums were hard to keep up with but I tried. I was particularly welcome when there was dirty work to do. The lot to the north of the Watson home at the corner of Elm and Ninth was a horse and goat lot. Carson owned two goats with harness and wagon. He and the gang organized the Columbia Goat Club. At first they held races on the university campus, around the old Academic Hall* columns, but were kicked off the campus because they were creating a disturbance, disrupting the dignity of the school. A track was then laid out at the rear of the E.W. Stephens home.* This home later became Stephens College's first Country Club.

"The Stephens home was the scene of many activities of the boys," Garth remembered. "One day it was decided that a nest of bumblebees was causing difficulties at the Stephens mansion outhouse, called more politely, 'the closet.' One of the boys produced a small cannon and aimed it at the bees, but then decided that Jimmy Garth was the most likely candidate for touching it off."

Little Jimmy, unsuspectingly, did as he was told, but failed to run. The bees zeroed in on him and he decided to take off for home across town. By the time he arrived, the bees had stung him from head to toe.

Dr. Watson, who examined and treated him for the stings, commented that Jimmy was "stung every place but the bottoms of his feet, and those feet must have been hitting the ground too fast for the bees to do any damage to them."

"Carson and R.B. Price were near the same age and were

9

inseparable," Garth said. "Samuel Laws was about five years older than Carson, and Edwin was the oldest boy in the family. The latter two brothers frequently took Carson and his 'hoodlums' cave exploring. The favorite place to go was the Hunt place, but to get there required the use of a wagon and horses. These were loaned to the boys by the Stephens family.

"Dr. Watson kept saddle horses to be used for his trips to visit his patients, and for his morning fox hunts, but at the time he did not maintain a buggy or a wagon. He used saddle bags, one on either side of his horse's withers, and in the bags were medical instruments and drugs, including arnica and turpentine for back ailments and sore muscles, and quinine for malaria."

On one occasion Carson and "R.B." got into the Doctor's saddle bags and purloined some turpentine. They then "doctored" a dog with it to see what would happen. Of course the dog reacted the way the boys hoped it would—perhaps with a little too much reaction. "The boys of that day had to manufacture their own activities," according to Price, "and sometimes their imagination took them into places, and made them do things they afterward regretted." Their activities caused Clara Watson some trouble."But she loved children and when she made crab-apple butter," Price said, "we were permitted to lick the spoon and crock."

Death in the Family

The boys' propensity for having fun and their ability to depend on themselves for their activities, led to the second tragedy* in the Watson household. Several of Carson's friends, all about thirteen or fourteen years old, arose about three o'clock one morning to watch the circus train come in and unload. The rain—a cold one—had already started to fall. But the boys were there well ahead of the arrival of the special, and they didn't mind the rain. The youngsters and the grown folks, numbering

10

well into the hundreds, were on hand to see the train arrive. When the show was shunted to the siding near the Wabash depot, and the animals began to descend from the cars, the younger elements of the crowd could hardly restrain themselves from shouting their approval.

The draft horses were the first unloaded. The wagons were next to be brought down the ramps. And the horses were hitched to the wagons for an immediate start to the Fair grounds. The ponies followed. There were a dozen of them, all sleek, well-rounded little fellows that indicated the excellent care and attention given them. A circus hand then descended from a car followed by a dozen or more dogs, which lined up much like sheep, all with their tails between their legs because they resented the rain. There were dogs of every color, size and breed, and they yelped and stretched their legs. Despite the rain, they were glad to leave the cramped quarters of the train.

Even though the boys were chilled to their bones, they watched the unloading for several hours. Carson was the first to leave. When he arrived home he had a fever, and his mother put him to bed. For six months he lingered, some days getting better and others worse, until finally he succumbed to spinal meningitis at the age of fourteen years on January 6, 1896.

Opal (Ward) Ashlock, a first cousin of Carson's recalled the gift of Carson's goat team that Dr. Watson presented to her brothers, John and Frank Ward. One goat, named "Nancy Hanks," was white-spotted and looked more like a dog than a goat. The other, named "Kitty," had long, curly white hair. Harness for the goats was a part of the gift, and the wagon had a tongue. "John and Frank hitched the goats to the wagon and had much fun with them," Mrs. Ashiock said. "I was an occasional rider in the wagon but I don't recall that I was much thrilled with the ride. However, the boys spent long and happy hours with the team of goats."

Edwin was saddened over the loss of his little brother, but the circus was never thought of as the cause of Carson's death, and there was no residue of bitterness. His mother, years later, wrote about the loss of her three children:

11

Oft in the stilly night,
When my eyes refuse to sleep,
Three little visitors come
With me the vigil keep.

The bright light of memory
Drives all darkness away,
And down the aisle of years
I see my children at play.

Dear Stella, Mattie and Carson,
My angel visitors three—
Come often with your magic wand
And wave it over me.

The Circus and Circus People

Edwin continued his long-time love affair with the circus and circus people. He was fond of pointing out that many circus companies were owned by brothers. He was friends with them all, including the Ringling brothers, the Gentry brothers, the trio of Sells brothers, the Cole brothers and others. Of the Sells brothers, William was Ed's favorite, and best-known of the brothers to the people of Columbia. William Sells, who died of gastritis in February 1908, had always said that "back in the '80's Columbia was the best show town in America." The Cole brothers brought to Columbia on May 10, 1906 the only living giant black camel known to man. Ed told and retold the story about the hunters for the Coles who were in the high, cold regions near the Lake of Lob Nor where they sighted a small number of wild camels. At the head of the herd was one towering far above the others in size and solid black in color. Never having seen a black camel before, and very few camels so large, the collectors became fired with the desire to capture the strange creature. They succeeded, but the chase was a lengthy and strenuous one, and before the prize was finally taken, several battles-royal were fought, with Black King Camel victorious in all but the last one.

12

Whenever the circus came to town, fathers were admonished in the *Tribune* by Ed "to remember the days when they were boys, and when they would have taken a good licking rather than miss a circus. They would also remember how their dads had given them not only enough money to get into the big tent, but enough to do all the side shows and buy peanuts and red lemonade."

"Show posters forced their gaudiness on the small boys' attention," wrote Ed, "causing restlessness until the day the big white top came into view. There they would see the red wagons, the flop-eared elephants, the ungainly camels, the equestrians and equestriennes, the death-defying stunts of the trapeze performers who sailed up to dizzy heights against the canvas, and the leap-for-life, just as advertised, the grand dive, and all the rest of—how would you like to be a boy again? Well, anyway, the children want to see it and you'll have to go along."

A circus was always good copy for Editor Watson. One such "copy" concerned the calliope player who "muffled his ears." He wore cotton wads stuffed into his ears and said; "If I didn't plug my ears this old melodian would drive me deaf." When asked if all calliope players did the same thing, he said: "I don't know if they all do, but I do."

With a hint of jealousy, Ed wrote about the newspaper that owned a circus:

Probably there are not two concerns in the world that own a newspaper and a circus. You can find editors who run their papers in connection with fried chicken farms, wood yards and a dozen other side lines, but it has remained for the Sells-Floto Co. to run a newspaper and a circus. Besides the big amusement concern, these people own the Kansas City Post in the city on the Kaw. How do you suppose it feels to be an editor and own a circus at the same time?

Then there's the story of the circus that reached Columbia and went broke. In 1910 when W.W. Garth was *Tribune* advertising manager, he told the story to Ed. The *Tribune* editor, ever alert for a good story for his news columns, reported it:

Jefferson Garth lived on a farm near Columbia in 1857 and upon the arrival of the circus, the owner permitted Garth's sons to sit on the front seat of the band wagon in the Grand Parade down Broadway. The circus gave its performance, but went broke, not having enough money to get to the next town. Mr. Garth did not forget the favor that the Circus Manager had extended to his sons, and he boarded the circus for three weeks, supplying feed for the horses and the elephant. The elephant had an excellent appetite. Those were hospitable times and nothing was said about board bills. Before the circus left, the Manager presented Mr. Garth with a very handsome English watch, including the key with which to wind it. It was gold, twice or three times the size of the average watch of the present day, and it would have brought $200 or more at that time.

Early Days

Sam Anderson, Friend

Sam Anderson, a friend of Ed's since college days, was on the first Missouri football team that played Kansas University. This was in 1891. The Tigers' initial effort at the game of football occurred the previous year, but they played only one game, and that was against Washington University in St. Louis, a 28-0 loss. Sam lived and boarded at the Watson home, and when Ed came from Texas to enter law school, the two renewed their friendship. In their mature years the two friends were together at many football games and fox hunts.

Anderson had been encouraged by an anonymous benefactor to come to Columbia from his home in St. Louis. He had no money, his parents were deceased, and he wanted to attend the University to play football. His desire realized, he eventually was able to claim the record for the longest drop-kick in Missouri's history, according to the testimony of his friends. Official records of the M. U. Athletic Department do not cover drop kicks, but the friends of Sam can be trusted for accuracy. Sam was also "considered by many as the best player on the team," as attested to by the *Columbia Herald* in a news story of the day.

In the first game he played against K.U. on October 31, 1891 the Tigers lost 22-8 at Exposition Park in Kansas City. Ed came from St. Joseph, where he was a reporter for the *Ballot,* to watch the unhappy defeat. The second game against K.U., played in the same park on Thanksgiving Day, Nov. 23, 1892, also was won by Kansas 12-4. In this game, the first touchdown was made by K.U., followed by the successful kicking of a two-point goal, and the score was 6-0.* A short time later in the

15

game, according to a news story in the *Columbia Herald,* "Jayhawk fullback W. H. Piatt and Missouri's quarterback, Sam Anderson, engaged in a fist fight, but officials restored order and gave Missouri an additional 25 yards and the ball." On a later play "Anderson fractured his collar bone and had to be carried from the field." Missouri finally made a touchdown, but Sam was not able to kick, and his substitute kicker missed. The score stood 6-4. K.U. then scored but the ball was called back because of Piatt's illegal tackle on D.L. Shawhan, who wrenched his knee and left the game. The Jayhawks again scored, kicked the two-point goal, and the final score read 12-4. Ed had gone to Fort Worth, Texas, in August to work on the *Star Telegram,* and was not able to return for the game. But this was the only Kansas game he missed in those many early years of watching the Tigers and the Jayhawks battle it out.

The Tigers won the third game and again Ed Watson's rugged friend was in the midst of the fray. But this time he confined his energies to the game rather than to the "extra-curricular festivities of fisticuffs,"as stated in the *Herald*. The game was played in Kansas City Nov. 30, 1893 before a crowd of some 5,000 at Exposition Park. Missouri's Eldred Harrison scored first after only two and a half minutes. Sam kicked an easy goal and the score was 6-0. The Jayhawks later made a touchdown but failed the goal. In the second half M.U. scored with Anderson again kicking the goal. No other scoring occurred and the Tigers won their first game from K.U. 12-4.

Years later Watson was fond of telling the story of how his friend had developed into the sure kicker of goals that he became. "When Missouri got a touchdown," Ed wrote, "the goal was a matter of course." Anderson had never played football until the fall of 1891. But he quickly adapted. His goal-kicking skill was acquired by long hours of patient practice. Ed wrote:

Some of the teams Missouri played had excellent goal-kickers, and Anderson resolved to acquire the ability to kick goals. He had a coal shed at the Anderson home, * with a door three feet square on the back side, at about the same distance from the ground as is the cross-bar on

16

the goal posts. With a small boy* as a helper to boot the balls back to him, Anderson practiced kicking the football through the coalhouse door, hour in and hour out. He acquired an uncanny sleight at the stunt, and could kick a football through a three-foot hole anywhere up to 20 yards. And then, the next fall, the results came.

In later years Sam owned a farm between Hallsville and Sturgeon. When visiting in Columbia he made the *Tribune* office his headquarters. His travels to Columbia were by train. Like Watson he remained unmarried, and through the years the two continued to be cronies. From time to time Sam kept Ed's dogs. Sam's farm was near Silver Fork Creek about half-way upstream from where it empties into Perche Creek, and this rough country north of Columbia was a favorite fox-hunting area for the two men.

* * *

Back to Law School

Edwin worked for E.W. Stephens at the *Herald* until he graduated in 1890. After nine years of Columbia newspaper work, learning to set type by hand, and doing a little of everything on the *Herald* including writing ads and news stories, he decided to take his talents out of town. He worked two years on the *St. Joseph Ballot* and two more years on the *Fort Worth Star-Telegram.* He then decided to change fields, returning to Columbia to enter law school. He received his LL.B. degree in 1897.

Ink In His Blood

After graduation he sought and won by a comfortable majority, the Democratic nomination for city attorney of Columbia. Then, as with all of Ed Watson's years in Columbia, the Democratic nomination was tantamount to election. The Republican party placed no ticket in the field and Ed received the unanimous vote cast in the general election. Prior to his election as city attorney he joined local attorney Wellington Gordon in the practice of law. At the expiration of his two-year term he refused to listen to the pleas of Democratic party leaders, and declined the race for a second term. He said that having to prosecute his friends in court was very distasteful, and he decided to go back to his first love, the newspaper business. Though his association with Gordon was pleasant he realized that "ink had gotten in his blood."

He went to Jefferson City as editor of the *State Tribune,* and to St. Louis in 1901 as a reporter with the *St. Louis Star.* Then he joined the *St. Louis Republic,* and later the *St. Louis Globe-Democrat.* For four years Watson held the tough job of a big city reporter. He spoke of the "rebuffs that must be taken with a resolve to forgive and forget and forge ahead." Doors were slammed in his face when he went to interview prominent citizens, and he was "thrown down stairs by an irate Irish tenement-dweller" when he tried to see the way the kitchen looked after Mike and his wife "had a drag-out fight." He had words with a "vindictive bar-tender" whose name he used in a story of a saloon fight. A lady whose picture was not returned was unhappy. The man whose "street and office number was printed incorrectly, was irate." And another man who talked to Ed for an hour "expecting to get a half-column of free advertising and then looked in vain for the story that the copy desk man had wastebasketed." These were some of the trials listed by Ed, but he still found the work satisfying.

Watson served his apprenticeship and was ready for the challenge of running his own newspaper. The opportunity came suddenly when his friend Ernest Mitchell, owner of the *Columbia Daily Tribune* died of typhoid on November 29, 1905.

At the time Ed was taking a Caribbean cruise with a friend who owned a sailing yacht. Margaret Waters, a personal friend

18

of Mitchell's widow, knew that her brother wanted to buy a newspaper, and she solicited the aid of her husband, Dr. H.J. Waters, then Dean of the University of Missouri College of Agriculture, and of her father, Dr. B.A. Watson. The two men arranged at the Exchange National Bank for a loan of $3,000. When Ed returned from his cruise on December 15, 1905, he took over $1,000 of the note and the newspaper. He listed himself next day as "Editor and Proprietor."* By the time his father died in 1918 the debt only had been reduced to $1,700, and it became a part of the B.A. Watson estate. Profits from *Tribune* operations were always "plowed back" into the paper.

Ed's first action as the new proprietor was to write a front-page editorial labelled "Announcement":

> *With this issue, title to the Columbia Daily Tribune passes from the estate of the late Ernest L. Mitchell to the undersigned, who will continue its publication as an afternoon daily newspaper.*
>
> *The Tribune will, in the future, as it has always done, endeavor to perform the cardinal functions of a newspaper—the upbuilding and advancement of the community in which it is published. Columbia and Boone County, their institutions, interests and people will at all times and under all circumstances receive the loyal support of the Tribune.*
>
> *The Tribune will be published as a newspaper for all the people. Endeavor will be made to chronicle in full the happenings in Columbia and vicinity, and in this regard sustain the standard set by the late, lamented editor and proprietor, Ernest L. Mitchell, in his management of the paper.*
>
> *The continued and continuous good will and patronage of subscribers and advertisers is solicited, and reciprocity is guaranteed as far as is in the power of the new management.*
>
> *E.M. Watson*
> *Editor and Proprietor*

On the following day, December 16, 1905, Ed advertised: "Boy Wanted at Tribune office to feed press and learn the printer's trade."*

This must have transported him in his thoughts back to his own boyhood days when he applied for a similar job offered by E.W. Stephens, publisher of the *Herald*.

The city of Columbia had a population of about "6,000 active citizens" in 1905. The town boasted of two music stores, two department stores, two "finely equipped colleges for girls (Stephens and Christian) and the University of Missouri with an enrollment of about 2,000 students. It had four hotels,* six churches—"better than the churches in larger cities," several churches for "colored people," three meat markets, seventeen grocery stores, three hardware stores, eighteen practicing attorneys, one full-time and three part-time men on the police force. There were three shoe stores—"where the latest styles in footwear are kept," a large electric light and water system, three large clothing stores, a "new and commodious" city hall, twenty-three practicing physicians, five doctors in dentistry, a healthy climate and beautiful scenery. It had one academy Columbia Normal—also known as Beasley Academy. It had an "excellent telephone system with connections to nearly all points of importance in the country," a "splendid" high school, three large lumber yards, two book stores, three saloons, three billiard halls, two cafes and three restaurants. There were enough boarding houses for everybody. Six large livery barns took care of transportation needs. A bowling alley provided "extremely popular" entertainment. The government furnished free mail delivery. There were two bakeries, two trunk lines—the Wabash and the M.K.& T., three drayage companies and a large brick manufactory with an increasing patronage. A handle factory "supplied the market of northwestern states." There was a wagon factory, "one of the largest flouring mills in the state," three weekly papers and ONE DAILY.

Watson at once began campaigns for many and varied

Old Academic Hall. A fire devastated this building on January 9, 1892, leaving only the six columns now historical landmarks on the M.U. campus.

Stewart Bridge built by Judge J.A. Stewart to join the University campus with his new subdivisions Westwood and Westmount. It connected Maple Street over the M. K.& T. tracks with Kings Highway, a street later changed to Stewart Road.

causes. He gave his attention to anything for the betterment of Columbia and Boone County. No hard-surfaced streets existed in the town, but Watson saw the need for them. A few of the streets were constructed from creek gravel or cinders from the city's own cinder pile at the Municipal Water and Light Plant. But most streets were dirt and deeply rutted. One early *Tribune* news story told of North Fourth Street that was "so bad that coal wagons can't deliver to colored people." This was Watson's first winter as owner of the paper.

A new subdivision, Westwood, had already been undertaken by Judge J.A. Stewart. It had a street impressively named Kings Highway.* At the time streets in the subdivision were all dirt.

Arguments were presented for various kinds of road materials, but Watson held out for "vitrified" brick. Always mindful of the duty of a newspaper to present other than its own side of an argument, he gave space to many leading citizens who disagreed with him. Marshall Gordon was one of those citizens who believed in saving money by using good creek gravel. In an editorial titled: "THE STREETS AND CREEK GRAVEL," Watson artfully and diplomatically gave the *Tribune's* side of the argument.

> *While the Tribune thinks that neither macadam nor gravel should be used in paving Broadway or any other business street of Columbia, it regards the suggestion made by Mr. Marshall Gordon, in his communication in this paper Saturday, as exceedingly valuable and sensible. Mr. Gordon points out the value of creek gravel for street building. Creek gravel, screened of the sand and dirt, and put down in the manner suggested in the communication would make an exceedingly hard and compact road, splendidly adapted for pleasant driving purposes, as well as able to stand wear and tear. Creek gravel is hard as flint and more durable than macadam. Of course it would have to be spread to the thickness of not less than a foot and compactly rolled. Some of the roads in foreign countries that have stood for many years are constructed of mountain gravel, which is practically the same as creek gravel of this vicinity. The material, however, would have*

*to be separated entirely from the sand and dirt, leaving
only the hard clean gravel.*

H.R. Richards, grocer, advertised that "owing to the extremely bad conditions of our streets at the present time we shall
make only two deliveries a day." And Ed commented:

*This street paving question is getting pretty close to home
when the butcher, the baker and the candlestick maker
can't deliver their wares on account of mud.*

Another grocer, George H. Roth, advocated brick paving
for all business streets. Watson asked:

*What street is going to have the honor of being the first
one paved? No small amount of honor will come to the
first street that has a fine surface of brick put upon it. It
looked as if University Avenue would lead off, but the
matter is not settled there. The city in some way should
honor the property owners who first put aside all trivial-
ities and succeed in having a street paved.*

Four months after Ed took over the *Tribune* he complained:

*And still not a contract for a paved street. Two months of
Spring are almost gone. Columbia has not grown tired of
the street paving question, has it? Let us all start kicking
again about the streets. If anything is going to be done, it
must be done immediately. We exhausted all discussion
about the kinds of paving; now let us have some of the
real article.*

On June 6, 1906, the *Tribune* came out with a banner head-
line: "JUDGE STEWART GETS CONTRACT FOR PAVING
BROADWAY." The bid of $19,612.50 was the lowest, and
Broadway was at last to be paved with "vitrified" brick from Sixth
Street to Tenth Street.

There were many board walks all over town at this time and
the council, as late as May 2, 1906, ordered plank walks to be

22

laid on Fay Street. On May 30 Watson began urging the building of "granitoid" walks.

The fact that Columbia was many years behind other towns in providing good sidewalks has in one respect proved beneficial to the town. It has given the city uniform walks, a very desirable thing for the community and a thing that adds much to the beauty of the place. There seems now to be no end of granitoid walks, and new walks are being put in all parts of town. The good work should go on.

Columbia's July 4 celebration came and went; the 1906 Boone County Fair also passed and still no work on the paving of Broadway. Watson commented:

A good many people are getting anxious to see a little dirt fly on Broadway or some of the other streets where paving is to be done. There are fears that it may be a cry of "wolf."

August 2 arrived and the *Tribune's* afternoon headline shouted: "MAKING DIRT FLY ON BROADWAY." The news story told of the "twelve teams and forty men" who started to work on Broadway that morning. It continued:

Mr. Stewart says the force will be increased both as to men and horses and that the work will be done very rapidly. The paving of the street will follow immediately as the ground is gotten ready, so that the street may be used as soon as possible. After grading, the rolling of the subgrade will be done and six inches of concrete will be first laid. On this will be placed two inches of sand. This will be rolled and the bricks will be placed on this. The bricks will be laid and an asphalt filler placed between them.

Ed Watson was not content to "let sleeping dogs lie." Seven days after the work started on Broadway, he wrote:

Verily, the day of street paving is upon us! Tuesday the council let the contract to pave Walnut Street. Broadway is being transformed. Columbia never takes two bites at a cherry. Whatever is attempted, is done brown. The Tribune predicts that miles of paved streets will be boasted within two years.

While the city of Columbia at last was working on its street-paving program, farmers in the area around Columbia also were busy.

Toll Roads

In June 1906, work began on the road to Curt Sutton's farm northeast of town, a distance of three and one-half miles. Oakland Road branched off Sutton's road, and plans were being made to gravel the road as far as Oakland Church. Several toll roads had been gravelled, including the Rocheport Gravel, the Fulton Gravel and the Ashland Gravel. None of these roads were in the best of shape, and in some instances, travelers refused to pay the toll. Patrons on the Ashland Gravel were "getting up in arms," according to the *Tribune* "because of the poor condition of the road." They refused to pay toll to the company that had been organized in 1898 and had a capital of $9,000. Other troubles came to the Ashland Road when gate keeper W.D. Morris resigned and "moved to town." The gate was a chain stretched across the road at the east bridge approach, south of the present-day Stadium Road bridge over Hinkson Creek.

Old Providence Road was about to be introduced into the good roads program by George Williamson, wealthy, bottom-land farmer of near McBaine. He offered to donate $1,000 to get the enterprise started. Williamson said "the farmers are tired of being isolated a large part of the winter, and all are satisfied that the value of their lands will be enhanced more than their donations by building the gravel road." Old Providence Road was the first improved road in the county. Practically all freight was shipped to Providence by river and hauled north to Columbia from the river village. At one time early-day citizens built a plank or "corduroy" road for the traffic. The old road followed the general direction of what has been named during the 1970's as Old Plank Road.

Watson was a "do-it-yourselfer," and he wrote an editorial on the newly-invented road drag:

The split-log drag is doing wonders in road improvement in many localities all over the state. One day's dragging insures an excellent road for months. Boone County farmers who live off the gravels should utilize the split-log. It makes the road work shorter by half.

In another editorial he explained:

Good roads cost money but they double the value of farmland because they bring the markets closer to the farmer. With better roads Boone County land would command better prices.

Old Trails Route

With the coming of the automobile, far-sighted citizens of Columbia, who were encouraged by Ed Watson's editorials, began to push for a cross-state highway from St. Louis to Kansas City.

The new road would follow the old Boone's Lick Trail to Columbia and push on west over the old Santa Fe Trail. The trails together were called the Old Trails Route. The first road built and paid for by the government of the United States was the National Road. In 1802 Congress set aside five per cent of the sales of public lands in Ohio for a road from the Atlantic to the Ohio River. It ran as a toll road from Cumberland, Maryland, to Wheeling, West Virginia. On it travelled the old stage coaches and wagon trains. Farther west the road continued through Ohio, Indiana and Illinois to the Mississippi River across from St. Louis. At St. Charles the National Road connected with the Boone's Lick Trail that led pioneer travelers to the beginining of the Santa Fe Trail at Franklin, Mo.

In 1804 two sons of Daniel Boone, Nathan and Daniel, manufactured salt at the springs across the river from a place the Indians called "Arrow Rock." The springs, named Boone's Lick, had been used as a source of salt by Indians and wildlife. The Boones and their companions were the only white men in the territory west of St. Charles. They boiled the spring water in huge kettles. The crude salt that formed the residue was floated in hollow logs down the Missouri River to be sold at the French village of St. Louis.

The cross-state highway was believed to offer immense benefits to every town it was to pass through, and many towns were bidding for the route. Three routes were possible, the Northern Route through Mexico, Moberly and other towns north of the river, the Southern Route through Jefferson City, Sedalia and other towns south of the river, and the Central Route that was to follow the general path of the Boone's Lick and Santa Fe trails. The latter was the route Watson was interested in. Several meetings were held along the proposed route but little organization resulted. Ed Watson thought that Columbia and Boone County "should get busy."

A meeting was held at Mineola. Columbians who attended included E.W. Stephens, N.T. Gentry, Walter Williams, J.A. Hudson, S.C. Hunt, T.S. Gordon, Ted Conley and E.M. Watson. This was in July 1911, and they met with others from Callaway, Montgomery and Warren counties.

Two factors were working for the Central Route, according to Watson. It was the shortest distance across the state. Also, neither of the other two routes could compare with it in historic interest and tradition. Mineola was an example of the historical interest. Van Bibber's Tavern was the most famous hostelry along the Boone's Lick Trail. Watson wrote:

The old Boone's Lick did not originally pass through Columbia but followed a route about seven miles north, running across Boone County near Browns Station and then in a line west to Howard County. Not the least interesting features of the Boone's Lick Road were the old taverns or inns. Here were the distributing points for information of

26

all kinds and here the travelers and antebellum politicians gathered in their cross-state trips on horseback or by stage.

One of the most famous of these old inns was Van Bibber's, located at Mineola, Montgomery County. The proprietor was a bonifice that was known the length of both the Boone's Lick Road and the Santa Fe Trail, and his hostelry was likewise famous. One of the mine host's firmest convictions was that history repeated itself and that all events, historical and otherwise, repeated themselves under exactly the same circumstances and with the same dramatis personae.

One day two prosperous young men travelers of more than ordinary intelligence stopped over-night at Mineola and put up at the inn. Van Bibber was quick to note their seeming prosperity, and after supper, he began descanting on his favorite topic. "Why," he observed to the travelers over one of his famous brews and the pipe, "Ten thousand years from this very minute we three will be sitting here in this very tavern enacting the parts we are now playing."

The next norning the travelers were up betimes, ate an early breakfast, mounted their horses and were just waving a goodbye to Van Bibber without mentioning aught of pay for their entertainment. Van Bibber reminded them of their oversight.

"Oh," laughingly responded one of the travelers, "We'll be along here again in ten thousand years and will pay you then."

"No you don't," said Van Bibber, "You're the two sons-of-guns who passed here ten thousand years ago and rode off without paying me."

Old Trails Celebration

Finally on August 18, 1911, the Central Route was selected by the State Board of Agriculture as the official cross-state highway between St. Louis and Kansas City. Celebrations were held in towns along the way. In Columbia, talks were given at the Boone County courthouse in the morning, and a parade was scheduled down Broadway for the afternoon. E.W. Stephens and William Hirth were the main speakers at the courthouse.

Two months later, the big celebration was held, with Columbia designated as the city to host Highway Dedication Day. The women of the Episcopal Church served hot, 50 cent dinners at the People's Restaurant, on Broadway near Tenth Street. Red, white and blue bunting decorated the old courthouse columns. Kansas City and St. Louis sent delegations of seventy-five cars each and were joined along the line by more than a hundred cars. Curtis Hill, state highway engineer, took a position at the head of the parade as official parade marshall. He assumed the job with the aid of a megaphone to direct the automobiles to their places in line. Watson commented that "there were some cold persons among the autoists, some dusty and dirty ones, some tired ones—but there was none who was not enthusiastic and none who was not happy."

Months passed, with Ed using all of his editorial wiles and power to get things done. On June 27, 1913, a "Good Roads Day" in Boone County was held, with every able-bodied man out with pick and shovel to work the roads. Some of the business men in town hired substitutes, and Ed Watson said "it reminded him of Civil War times when Union sympathizers who were drafted could hire a substitute to be shot at." He agreed that "the business men have more spirit, but it is altogether probable that the sub would do several times more work by sundown."

Pick and Shovel

When the end of the day came, the 44-year-old editor of the *Tribune* was glad it was over. He offered for sale his second-hand pick and his second-hand shovel:

They cannot possibly be used in the making of a country daily, else The Tribune would not even consider disposing of them. The Tribune is a great stickler for consistency. It agrees with the gentleman who made the assertion that it is a jewel. The Tribune also believes the sentiment expressed in the Good Book when it says "Be ye doers of the word and not believers only." The Tribune has always had a good deal to say about the benefits of tne State Highway and of good roads generally, so when the call was made for volunteers it "signed up" to do a day's work, as many others did. It might be said in this connection that many didn't deliver the goods, their only contribution being the free distribution of advice as to how roads should be built.

But back to business. The tools above mentioned are practically new, only having been used one day. The Tribune, however, doesn't wish to misrepresent the condition of these tools in any way. Just to be "on the level" with all who may rush to this bargain counter, it will say that the day was the longest one that ever burdened the calendar. At 10 o'clock it seemed noon, and at 12 o'clock it seemed "taking out" time. The pick came in rude contact all day with what was the Rocheport Gravel Road, but is now the State Highway. The point is considerably blunted and the edge on the other horn of the pick shows a number of gaps. Neither is the shovel what it was yesterday morn when purchased, all of which goes to show that the Tribune was no sluggard in the labor of bettering the State Highway, but ate its bread in the sweat of its face during all the sizzling torridity of yesterday.

With this candid statement of the condition of the Tribune's pick and shovel, we offer them for sale . They are functionless around a newspaper office, unless some aggrieved reader should come in to lick the editor for telling the truth. We would never have acquired them, but for the spark of conscience that made us choose the ruck rather than enlist with the banner carriers who traversed the route in automobiles and did the whoopin' up.

A few days later Watson wrote an editorial entitled: "The Farmers' Recompense." He wrote:

The Boone County farmer who assists in the betterment of the State Highway now, by the donation of a team or two and some labor, will reap the reward before a great while when the expenditure of money on the great National Highway begins. This ocean-to-ocean highway is certain of construction and it will follow the official State Highways, which are largely made up of old trail routes over which early civilization was blazed.

Watson was right. The ocean-to-ocean highway was eventually constructed, but there were many difficulties that had to be overcome along the way. Toll roads had been the best roads in and out of Columbia since the late 1800's, but they were constructed for wagon traffic. Indeed, toll charges for automobiles had not been built into the toll road contracts. They were finally authorized by the legislature, effective in June 1911. The Ashland Gravel Road Company began charging automobiles four cents a mile for round trips over their road, half of what the new law allowed them to charge.

One of the chief stumbling blocks to the cross-state highway aside from the Mineola hills, was the lack of a bridge at Arrow Rock, Glasgow or Boonville. The state organization of the Daughters of the American Revolution suggested "that a ferry could be used advantageously in crossing the river, that a bridge was not at all necessary and that the lack of one should not interfere with choosing the best and most historic route for the cross-state road."

Eventually, ferries were installed at all three of the locations. But Boonville started a subscription stock sale for building a bridge, and this was the deciding factor in the decision to take Highway 40 across the river at Boonville.

Missouri State Patrol

The new cross-state highway brought maintenance problems. It was suggested by the State Highway Commissioner that "a patrol car should visit all parts of the road in Missouri at intervals. Watson agreed that the suggestion should be acted upon and that "a patrol car would serve to advertise the highway with passing motorists by means of a sign on the sides of the car reading Old Trails Highway Patrol."

"Incidentally," wrote Watson, probably recalling his own highway work, "the patrolman, if a practical road worker, could carry a pick and shovel and do much small repair work."

In following the old Trails Route the new highway faced its biggest obstacle in Mineola hills. W.B. Cauthorn, Boone County Engineer, proposed that the new road circumvent the hills, going north—if Mr. Graham, the owner of Graham Cave and the adjoining land, would agree. A year later Mineola hills were still in the news and Ed wrote:

Suggestion has again brought the Mineola hills near a solution but it will take dollars and work, and plenty of both, to make the hills travelable. The poor old Mineola hills have been lashed to death with talk but they still loom up majestically in front of the traveler.

In 1926 the new concrete highway No. 2—later renamed Highway 40, and still later Interstate 70—snaked its way down the east Mineola hill to the town of Mineola in the valley and then up again toward the opposite hill to the west. It was a slow road to travel, but it beat climbing over and around boulders.

The Boonville bridge over the Missouri River was built several years earlier. Assisting the drive for money to build the bridge, Ed wrote:

Not since the contemplated removal of the University from Columbia and the building of the two railroads, con-

necting this city with trunk line roads, has there been an enterprise that should more engage the concern of the people of Boone County and Columbia and enlist greater financial support than the proposition to build a bridge at Boonville. It involves the matter of whether Columbia is to remain on a trunk thoroughfare traversing Missouri, or is to be relegated to a location on a highway which will be of minor importance—one that is simply a feeder to the big one that is to be state and government-built and state and government-maintained.

History was always a favorite subject of Ed's. He first wanted the cross-state highway to follow the Old Trails route because of its historical significance. But in time he changed his views:

In presenting the claims of the Old Trails Route to the state highway commission for designation as a primary road, there are two, only two, paramount effective wedges to be driven. These are: Number of people served as traffickers, and second, the relationship of the road to marketing.

The highway commission cannot be appealed to effectively on sentimental grounds; it cannot be expected to designate a road simply because Daniel Boone travelled the road a hundred years ago.

Headquarters for Insurance

While street-paving and good roads were high on Watson's list of projects, there were many others, including the cutting of weeds, and the encouragement of insurance industries to pick Columbia for their headquarters.

He urged architects and builders to make sure buildings were fireproof. This was a favorite subject for editorials throughout his life. His first drive was for a fireproof courthouse. He thought that the city council should add a second fireman to the one-man fire department, and buy a fire engine. The city had

Columbia High School, Eighth and Rogers streets, which has been added to and is now Jefferson Junior High School. The dedication of the building, erected at a cost of $110,000, was held March 1, 1911.

Daniel Boone Tavern, now the City-County building, built in 1917, was named for the long-rifle pioneer. Ed Watson had sought for eleven years, without success, a memorial or a statue to Daniel Boone. A few years after Ed's father died in 1918, he and his mother moved into the hotel where he continued to live several years after his mother died in 1927.

used volunteers as fire-fighters and these men were "willing but inadequately trained."

Columbia also needed a new high school. But it should be a FIREPROOF high school. In editorial after editorial Ed talked about building the new high school in a central location and it was finally revealed that his idea of a central location was "at some point a block north of Broadway and within a block or two of the courthouse." Four months later he had changed his mind about the location:

Several months ago the Tribune suggested the erection of a centrally located, up-to-date high school. The school board is advertising for bids for property upon which to locate the new school, but the Tribune believes that the handsome new high school building should be erected on the location of the old. * While it may not now be centrally located, it will be, ten years from now, as Columbia is growing faster north, northwest and west than in other directions.

In April 1910 the school board voted to build the high school on the old site, and Watson complimented them for "acting wisely."

Chautauquas Were Big

Chautauquas were popular in the early 1900's and Watson gave editorial backing to William Hirth, the prime mover for bringing them to Columbia. The events, never financially successful, placed the sponsors $1,000 in debt by the fourth year. The twenty sponsors paid off the debt and Ed wrote an obituary:

The Chautauqua bee seems to have "dropped softly as a star from out the summer sky" of this community. They still flourish in other places, but failed financially here after three honest attempts had been made by public spirited

citizens to make a permanent institution out of the events.
The financial finale was disastrous. The reason for it was
that entertainments of the nature of Chautauquas have
for years been the order of events in Columbia. In fact
attractions superior to those ordinarily heard upon such
occasions, come to Columbia every week during the
school year. They, accordingly, have long ceased to be
novelties. Therefore, the passing of the Chautauqua in
Columbia.

Another project that failed was a belated drive made by
some citizens to save the old courthouse. The drive was started
before Watson bought the *Tribune,* but he was on the scene in
time to exert his influence to save the courthouse columns. He
told of the "sentimental regard for the memories that hang about
the historic old courthouse that would prompt many to preserve
it." But he admitted that the old building had served its day. Its
going is "another milestone on Boone County's roadway of progress," he said. Bricks from the old building were transported to
the site of Fyfer's new apartment building,* Broadway and Hitt
Street.

"It is hoped," wrote Watson, "that the county court will decide to leave the old columns as a monument to the past and its
sturdy pioneer deeds." "The columns," he continued, "should
be furnished with massive bases like the University pillars and a
terrace constructed about them. It would be an artistic complement to the jewel of the University quadrangle and would re-
lieve, in a large measure, the barren effect at the head of Eighth
Street, which the removal of the old courthouse will produce."

Daniel Boone Statue

The cudgels for a Daniel Boone statue were taken up by Ed,
and although Dr. Ozias Paquin* had made the original suggestion that a statue to the early day pioneer be assigned to a sculp-
tor, Ed was more persistent in pursuit of the goal. He started his

campaign only two months after becoming Editor and Proprietor of the *Tribune,* and for eleven years, he continued his drive at intervals until the building of the Daniel Boone Hotel was assured in early 1916:

> *What better monument could be erected to Daniel Boone than the five-story hotel planned for Columbia? Standing on the old Boone's Lick Road itself, fronting the pathway over which the long-rifle pioneers pressed forward in their conquest of the wilderness, it will be a fitting marker to the memory of the man for whom the old county is named.*

> *What though the deer trail is now paved with brick, and a town of 14,000 inhabitants stands on the spot where a few log cabins and a frontier blockhouse marked the first settlement? That the deeds of those parlous times still live in memory, that Daniel Boone means much to the great Boone's Lick country which he and his intrepid companions snatched from the savages, can be impressed on the visitor in no more suitable way than by naming the big, modern, fire-proof metropolitan hotel after Daniel Boone.*

YMCA Dorm for Men

A campaign was conducted to build a YMCA dormitory for M.U. men students prior to Ed's taking over the Tribune, and he had a few comments to make concerning the help, or lack of it, from the local citizenry:

> *It was nothing but absolute truth when the board of trustees of the students YMCA building declared that the citizens of Columbia had done very little for the building. Only fifty citizens have subscribed.*

Ed's brother-in-law, Dean Waters, was on the board of trustees, along with Walter Williams, President R.H. Jesse, Prof.

John Pickard, W.B. Nowell, H.H. Banks and E.W. Stephens. These men were able to get the project sufficiently funded to start building in early 1907, but unable to complete it, at a cost of $40,000, until August, 1909. The largest contribution, $15,000, was made by A.H. Jones of Hallsville.

A Town That Does Things

When the president of the Hamilton-Brown Shoe Company set a bonus of $50,000 as the price for bringing a factory to Columbia, Ed Watson said: "This amount can be raised and will be raised."

After it was raised he editorialized:

This grand old town is already being rewarded for its enterprise by papers elsewhere in Central Missouri. They are telling of the city's success in securing the shoe factory, * and adding that Columbia is a town that does things.

A Good Convention Town

Columbia could not only "do things," but it was a town ideally located for conventions. Ed wrote:

There is every reason why Columbia should attract many conventions annually. It is centrally located, is easy of access from every part of the state, although no trunk line railroad passes through it. There is more to interest visitors here than can be offered by any town or city in Missouri. All that is needed to make Columbia ideal for this purpose is a commodious hotel building such as is being contemplated at the present time. With this complement to its other advantages, Columbia is the logical convention town of Missouri.

Spitting Where Listeth

War was declared by the city council on sidewalk spitters and Ed commiserated with the spitters, but at the same time, supported the city fathers in their efforts to enforce the law. He editorialized on the practice as the "Passing of an Inalienable Right:"

Until the city council last night put a ban on the practice and the privilege, a man spat where he listeth. It recked not the time, the place nor the occasion, the Columbian expectorated wherever or whenever his fancy or his inclination dictated. But a new order of things has arisen. This inalienable right has been taken from him by the City Fathers. Expert expectorating will now, no doubt, become a lost art. There are many citizens of Columbia who have rare accomplishments in this line. Facility and accuracy in this requirement does not come naturally. Persistent perseverance and strict attention to detail is the price of it. There are those in Columbia who can expectorate through a crack at an incredible distance with unerring accuracy. A cuspidor ten or fifteen feet away has no terrors for these knights of the strong and supple lip. As suggested above, this order of things must necessarily pass with the enforcement of the ordinance just become a city law. Instead of masculinity able to spit a wide and graceful parabola, we will have a puny generation not capable of expectorating over its chin.

All of the above has its melancholy phases and is sad to contemplate, but the new ordinance is probably all for the best. It will prohibit the courthouse loafers on the east side of the courthouse portico from firing willy-nilly into space and oftentimes, when the wind is in the west or southwest, right into the faces of whomever may be coming the wrong direction. These incidents will be missed both by the loafers and pedestrians, but the occurrences never were necessary.

In the meantime, everyone should be coaching himself to expectorate in the gutter, if he must needs expectorate at all, or lay himself liable to making a contribution of one dollar and the trimmings to the city's exchequer.

Why a Humane Society?

As mentioned, an important part of Ed's life included dogs and horses, and it was natural that he would, in his first year as editor of the *Tribune,* call Columbia citizens' attention to the need for a Humane Society. In an editorial he wrote:

Cases are seen on the streets every day that need the attention of a humane officer and the salutary effects of a court fine. Horses with galled shoulders and sore backs are worked without protest from anyone. Jaded animals are whipped and beaten unmercifully by unfeeling drivers. Horses are left hours at a time standing on the streets in freezing slush and snow. Aside from the laws of humanity forbidding these practices, there are statutes that prohibit them. The law provides for the punishment of those who are brutes enough to mistreat a dumb brute. A humane society should be organized to invoke this law.

Fox Hound Music

Watson's love for horses held equal rating with his enjoyment of the "music" of his fox hounds. Throughout his life he revelled in the chase. As most hunters of his time he enjoyed hunting at night. His father was the exception, preferring to rise early in the morning to take his dogs on a hunt. Boarders who lived at the Watson home recalled being awakened by the blast of the fox horn which Doctor Watson sounded to call his dogs, and after they were gathered, the Doctor headed his horse south toward the general direction of what is now College Avenue and Stadium Road.

Like his father, Ed was at ease out-of-doors. He loved to walk along the banks of streams, or sit around a campfire on a hill with other fox hunters, identifying the voice of each dog, telling stories of other hunts, and enjoying the companionship of like-minded men. His hounds, put up at the homes of friends throughout Boone County, were "blooded," but he also had a fondness for "mutts" and "strays."

Jiggs

One odd "stray," a British bulldog, ambled into the *Tribune* office one day in 1924 and attached himself to Watson and his long-time associate, City Editor Hollis Edwards. The dog, given the name "Jiggs"* by his new masters, was ugly, bow-legged, underslung and old, but wherever either of his new masters went he tried to follow, first one and then the other. He slept part of the day in the small space between Watson's rolltop desk and Edward's news-copy table, the latter a flat top supported by huge legs from a dismembered grand piano.

Jiggs possessed one bad trait that finally did him in. He had an ingrained habit of fighting, and toothless though he was, he took on all comers, regardless of breed or size.

It was finally decided that he was causing too much trouble in a busy newspaper office, and more to the point, he was getting licked every time he fought. Sadly, Jiggs would have to go. A friend, Paul Bell, offered to keep him at his livery barn on East Ash Street and Water Street.* The old dog spent the last several months of his life in peace, on a diet of milk and eggs, provided by his new master. Jiggs died August 9, 1926 and was memoralized next day in a *Tribune* news story:

OLD "JIGGS" WELL KNOWN
BULLDOG DIED YESTERDAY

"Jiggs," the old, underslung British bulldog who(sic) was a familiar figure around the Tribune for more than a year, died yesterday. "Jiggs" was old and almost toothless yet

he never stopped fighting, and for this reason he was taken from the Tribune office and given to Paul Bell. Mr. Bell kept the old dog at his barn on Ash, and for several months had fed him nothing but milk and eggs. He was buried on the banks of Flat Branch.

Happy Hooligan

Another dog that was given an obituary in the paper was Happy Hooligan, J.W. Sapp's pet dog and the "friend of every friend of the County Treasurer."

Happy Hooligan died Saturday. He was a yellow dog, but only in color. Inside his yellow coat beat a heart that was faithful, affectionate, and true to his master. He was the constant companion of Mr. Sapp. Wherever Hooligan was seen, it was a safe wager that his master was somewhere near. Two or three weeks back, Hooligan began to droop and before he died, his plump body became emaciated to thinness. He could scarcely walk or wag his abbreviated tail, but he insisted upon following his master as he had done for years. The last two or three days he was unable to do so and Saturday he was found dead. What malady took Hooligan away is not known, but it is presumed that something he ate poisoned him by degrees.

Old Jim

Dogs were not the only animals mourned with obituaries. There was "Old Jim" at Prathersville:

"Old Jim," the gin horse at Davis & Watson's coal mine, five miles north of Columbia, dropped dead Saturday afternoon just after he had drawn up a load of coal from the mine. "Old Jim" died in harness after a service of about ten years at the mine in question. Jim was said to be the best "gin" horse in the county. He had wonderful intelligence and the men at the mine say he could understand

40

anything that was said to him about manipulating the gin. He would stop at a word, turn around, lower a load back into the mine or do anything else required. The miners spoke of Jim as if he were an individual and so great was his intelligence that they regarded him almost as human. If any showed a disposition to abuse Jim, the old horse had a champion in every miner who had worked with him. Jim's ending was sudden and there was a note of sincere sorrow in their voices when they recounted the intelligent things that he used to do.

Old Bet

Then there was Bet, the family mule owned by A.J. Estes:

"Old Bet," the cornerstone of A.J. Estes' fortune, is dead. Bet had been on the retired list for six years, grazing on blue-grass pasture and eating her fill at the barn. Up until a few years ago Bet was as good a mule as ever stepped, despite her years, but age told.

"I bought that mule from John W. Keene for $125, twenty-eight years ago, and she was a three-year-old at the time," said Mr. Estes today. "Bet was a good mule. I plowed with her the first crop of corn I ever put in for myself. I bought Bet and went in debt for the other mule, and I sold that other mule several years afterward. Bet is buried on my place, and I am going to put a marker of some sort on her grave."

Prince the Firehorse

Deceased pets were given most of the attention in *Tribune* print, but live animals were also honored, including Old Prince, the horse belonging to the city that was about to be ordered shot by the city council on account of old age. Prince was reported frisky and strong, and was taken down to Mayor Clinkscales' pasture. He was turned loose on the grass and hadn't anything to do but eat for four months. The council voted against ending Prince's life and agreed to "sell the old fire department horse to the highest bidder."

Pete and Dick

Another news story was head-lined INTELLIGENT MULES:

The Boone County Milling Company has a pair of gray mules that are unusually intelligent, even for mules. They are big fellows, well mated and go by the names of Pete and Dick. They are staid, business-like animals and know exactly what is expected of them. On the round of delivering flour and other products to the regular customers of the mill, they need no driving. They walk solemnly along with a big load and draw the wagon as nicely alongside the curb as if they were guided there by a driver. They can make a good turn and describe a circle with the big wagon perfectly.

This morning, after the wagon had been filled at the mill, there was some delay in starting on the round of delivery. Pete and Dick thought the delay too long and started out on their own hook. They went up to E.R. Gribble's, the first stop, and left the wagon wheels not over three inches from the curb and not a foot from the place where their driver, Arthur Strawn, usually halts them. Arthur was helping load another wagon and didn't notice that his team was gone until it was half-way to Gribble's. He then came up and unloaded the purchase. Arthur is proud of his gray pets and tells some good stories of their intelligence.

Frequently, small pets were lost, and always earned a story in the *Tribune,* especially if they belonged to children. One such story was headlined LOST, A TABBY CAT:

42

This isn't an ordinary want ad, of some one with the commercial desire to buy or sell, but the plaint of a little girl to recover something that is dearer to her than dollars and cents. So every one who remembers what the wringing of a little one's heart means to the little one, be on the lookout for a gray-striped cat, about half-grown.

Lost: A gray-striped cat about half grown. Finder can get reward. Mary Frances Wildman, Westmount.

DR. SCHLEEF'S DOG HAS HIS DAY was the headline about a Llewellyn setter that woke his master to warn him about a fire.

Licking his master's face as he lay asleep in his apartment about 4:30 o'clock yesterday morning at 910-A Broadway, Dr. O.F. Schleef's setter, "Strode," gave an alarm of fire that in all probability saved thousands of dollars worth of property in the business section of Columbia. After being awakened, Dr. Schleef telephoned the fire department that T.C. Bonner's Bakery in the rear of 916 Broadway was all ablaze, and after a few minutes fight with the fire, it was extinguished with a loss of between $400 and $500, which fortunately was covered with insurance.

Yesterday morning Strode came to his master's bedside, poked his cold nose into his face, whined and then sniffed significantly. Dr. Schleef was about to scold him and send him back to his pallet when he detected the odor of smoke. He arose at once and walked to the front windows on Broadway. Instead of following him, Strode ran to the rear windows of the apartment, placed his paws on the sill, giving every indication that something was wrong. Dr. Schleef then went to the rear windows of the apartment and saw the whole of Bonner's Bakery ablaze. The alarm of fire quickly followed.

It is said "every dog has his day," but Strode Schleef's Day will be every day, for all the merchants in the block will gratefully remember and laud his intelligence long after he is in the Elysian Fields of dogdom.

Harry Clay

Along about the time Ed was bringing to a close his first year at the university, his father purchased from Dr. A.W. McAlester a sorrel suckling colt. It was by the McAlester imported horse, "Hirsch," and his dam was a standard bred mare. He carried the name "Harry Clay," and was used by Dr. Watson and family for twenty-three years as the family horse. On April 18, 1908, three years after Ed bought the *Tribune,* Harry died, presumably from being overheated. Ed wrote a short obituary:

> *Though past the age when most horses cease to be of service Harry was still a good animal and would have lived several years longer had he not become overheated. He was possessed of unusual stamina and intelligence and while high spirited, was sensible and gentle. There is genuine grief in Dr. Watson's family over Harry's death.*

Chase of Reynard

Horses had been used in England in the "Chase of Reynard," but our democratic forefathers from England soon dropped most of the formalities of the chase, including the red uniforms and the riding crops, but they continued their appreciation of dogs with good breeding lines. The chase was brought into Callaway and Boone counties from Virginia and Kentucky and had many devotees of the sport throughout the 1800's. But fox hunting fell into a slump along about the early 1900's. Watson had owned the *Tribune* less than six months when he complained in an editorial note that the "sport had lapsed into a state of innocuous desuetude." But there was "some hope of revival," he said, "under the leadership of of D.B. Hulett, Haden Bright and Philip Elkins." Concerning this "revival of the sport," he wrote:

> *Most every night, when the wind and weather and other conditions are propitious, these votaries of the "sport of*

The "Pinnacles," a geological oddity left by the glaciers, is the site of a beautiful resort area twelve miles north of Columbia on Silver Fork Creek. In 1906 a health "sanitarium" was established in this "high and healthful part of Boone County" by Dr. J.T. Gaines, because of "the pure water and healthful surroundings."

A Fox Hunt. Ed Watson enjoyed the "music" of the foxhounds and also the companionship with other devotees of the chase.

kings" may be seen wending their way toward the Grindstone hills, to the wildwoods, to the Bethel Church neighborhood and to other haunts of wily Reynard, followed by the pack of hounds which they are getting together.

And, by the way, this pack promises to be one of the best in Boone County before the above mentioned gentlemen cease their efforts in getting the choicest hounds that can be procured. Any that show the white feather are quickly given away or put where they are of no more bother. Some of their pack, in conjunction with that of John Johnson, who lives four miles southwest of town, can give any pack in the county an argument. In company with the latter, they make occasional visits to Gene and Frank Scott, to Tom Rees, and R.L. and S.P. Keene and others who take delight in hearing the music of a pack of hounds.

The majority scoff and tell bewhiskered old tales about the "music," as it is sometimes called derisively, but the ears of these scoffers are not properly attuned. They can probably not hear "the music of the spheres," but it is all about them just the same. Your votary of fox hunting accordingly has sincere pity for the man who asks him "What d'ye see in fox hunting?" The fox hunter is always too considerate to point out that there is something lacking in the makeup of the interrogator. But he knows the ecstacy that the music of the pack brings and he doesn't envy the lover of grand opera and other classical music one whit. And practically all fox hunters enjoy good music. The faculty they have of enjoying more kinds of music than the average mortal is something additional that has been vouchsafed them by a kind providence.

Elk Lick Springs

If fox hunting had "lapsed into desuetude" in 1905, as Watson lamented, it received quite a boost in 1907 when the Central Missouri Fox and Wolf Hunting Club was organized. Boone Countians, including Ed and his father, Eugene and Frank Scott,

45

Derby Bass, Lee Forbis, A.L. Ferguson and J.L. Harris joined the club and for many years attended the annual meeting which in the beginning was held at Elk Lick Springs, near Nelson in Saline County.

Tents were erected, a restaurant was made available on the grounds, and transportation from the Missouri Pacific depot at Nelson was furnished "at reasonable rates." The meet was all week long and hunts were held each day. As many as 200 hounds were entered in the meet. Watson recorded the event:

> The area around Nelson is ideally located for chasing Reynard, being in a sparsely settled part of the country which affords excellent cover for foxes. The section is also a good one to run over. Thursday is Ladies Day and a great many from the surrounding country, Sedalia, Boonville and other towns, always attend.
>
> Lee Forbis took with him three fox hounds, Spot, Hanger and Long Tom, all of which are by Bummer, a well known fox hound that Adolphus Scott bought from William Senor. Bummer has practically all the best fox hound crosses in Boone County in his breeding and is the sire of many good dogs. On both his sire's and his mother's side he runs back to the English hounds that the late James Duncan and C.B. Gordon imported from England a number of years ago.

Choteau Springs

In May 1919, the club moved its meet about half-way between Fayette and Glasgow, to an area, according to Watson, that was "one of the finest parts of Missouri." Later the same year E.A. Windsor held an unsponsored meet on his property at Choteau Springs west of Boonville. Windsor "threw open his cottages at the springs for the accommodation of such hunters who wished to bring their wives and daughters to the meet."

46

Rock Bridge

In October 1922, the Boone County Fox Hunters Association was organized and held its first meet in the Rock Bridge area. A *Tribune* headline stated:

FOX HUNTERS FARED BADLY LAST NIGHT

Weather conditions were not favorable for the fox hunt last night until after 10 o'clock. A slight wind blowing from the northwest prevented dew falling, thus depriving the hunters of dampness, a necessary condition for successfully running a red fox. On account of this the dogs were unable to track Reynard.

The wind ceased blowing at about 10 o'clock and by 11 o'clock sufficient dew had gathered to make hunting conditions fairly good in the woods and pastures, but indifferent in plowed ground. A fairly good chase was enjoyed for about an hour, but the fox was a wily one, and after three bad faults, secured a run in the hounds which finally caused them to lose him altogether, although some of the dogs were still working on his trail at 2:20 o'clock this morning.

Four dogs, which are known to cry nothing but a fox track, were sent out in charge of four of the hunting party. They went east of the Billy Reyburn place and ten minutes after, struck a fox track on Gans Creek, which runs through the Reyburn place.

The other hunters held their dogs in hand until a blast from one of the hunter's horn gave the signal that Reynard's track had been struck. Practically all the dogs were then released and all went to the assistance of the four dogs which were working on the track. It was so dry, however, that it was impossible for the hounds to follow the trail to a "jump." They worked over two hours and were finally called off, and another woods to the west

*near the Fortney cemetery was tried. Here a track was
also struck with the same result.*

*It was then nearly 11 o'clock and considerable dew had
fallen. The dogs were again taken east of the Reyburn
place, and this time they succeeded in jumping a fox.
Spirited running was had for a while, but three losses
within about three quarters of an hour enabled Reynard
to put so much distance between him and his pursuers
that his track finally became too cold to follow successfully, the fox being aided by the wind, which had again
arisen.*

*Anyone desiring to hear the chase tonight should take the
Providence road, turn east where the road forks at what
is known as the Jake Johnson place, and then proceed
on south over the hill when Rock Bridge is reached.*

*Intimations have been made that there was some crap
shooting and moonshine in evidence near the grounds
last night, Sheriff Brown will be asked to send a deputy to
the grounds tonight. The gentry was not invited to the
hunt and their absence is more than desired.*

Pups in the Press Pit

Many hunters around Boone County kept Watson's dogs.
They included Brown Conklin, Sam Anderson, Clyde Hopper,
"Coon Dog" Sapp, and a tenant farmer, Luke Bass, who lived
on Scott Island in the Missouri River across from Providence.
M.D. Jett, long-time business manager of the *Tribune* who with
other employees, always referred to Watson as "the Boss," told
of the Boss' practice of bringing pups to the *Tribune* to be cared
for.

"I spread newsprint on the floor of the press pit, and turned
the pups loose," said Jett. "Although they remained under the
press during the press run, and there was plenty of noise over-
head, it didn't seem to bother them. They got used to the racket,
I suppose."

48

One of the stories the Boss enjoyed telling was that of the fox hunter who took his dogs and a friend on a hunt south of town. He had been bragging to his friend about the sound his dogs would put out when on a tight trail of a fox.

They arrived at a hilltop spot where they turned the dogs loose and pretty soon a hot run began. The proud owner exclaimed to his friend: "Listen to that—hear that music?" The friend tried to listen and finally said: "I can't hear the music for the racket of them damn dogs."

Grandpa in Terrapin Neck

Another story concerned the venerable fox out in the Terrapin Neck* neighborhood. After some years had elapsed, the fox had been nick-named "Grandpa." His den was on Captain Lowrey's place, and the old red fox had been furnishing amusement for fox hunters in the "Neck" for years. Ed tells the story:

On Thanksgiving Day the Daly boys and some other fox hunters took their annual hunt. They went over to where Grandpa lived and jumped him immediately. For an hour old Reynard furnished fine amusement and the pack was running in a bunch. Sam Rummans was hunting birds and rabbits, and when Grandpa ran close to him he turned him over with a load of buckshot. This is the cardinal sin in the eyes of a fox hunter and if Mr. Rummans hadn't been a neighbor, there would have been trouble.

Nobody knew how old Grandpa was. County Clerk L.T. Searcy declares that he had run him many a time 15 or 20 years ago. When the old fox was examined he was found to have one eye out, an ear gone and his head was white with age. Despite his years, Grandpa always made a good race for three or four hours even in his declining years. In his prime this old red scorned to take a hole under eight or ten hours, even with the packs of the Scotts, the Dalys and the Lowreys after him.

49

There is genuine regret among the fox hunters of Terrapin Neck over Grandpa's passing. What makes it more regretable is the ignoble manner in which he met his end. There would have been great glory and satisfaction to Grandpa, no doubt, to have had for his requiem the music of the pack and the shouts of the hunters, but to be shot by a bird hunter and to have the crack of a shotgun for his death knell must have been a bitter ending for Grandpa. He has the sympathy of all genuine fox hunters.

A Fox at a Wedding

The chase gets into the blood of the true hunter. Even an important occasion such as a wedding proved not good competition at the Bea-Hall nuptials east of town. Ed wrote:

A wedding this morning offered the unusual attraction of a fox hunt, in addition to the nuptials and a beautiful wedding feast. The fox hunt, however, was not planned as part of the festivities.

Miss Katie E. Hall, daughter of Mr. and Mrs. W.A. Hall of four miles east of town, was married to Roy Bea, son of Willis Bea. Rev. W.S. St. Clair of Columbia, performed the ceremony.

The fox hunt came about in this wise. John White, a bachelor, and one of the fox hunters of the neighborhood, was one of the guests and had brought his favorite hound with him. Before the ceremony, someone heard hounds giving tongue and looked out of the window in time to see a fox racing across a field about two hundred yards from the house. As all fox hunters know, there is not time to be lost in such a case. Mr. White ran out in the yard, without his hat, and started his hound after the fox. Three other hounds raced past in full cry. The guests turned out to watch the fox, which soon disappeared.

The preparations were about completed for the marriage ceremony and everyone was watching for the entrance of the bride, when the fox came back into view, doubling on his course, and running warily in an effort to shake off the hounds, which were hanging to the trail and running in great style.

Guests kept one eye out of the window for the fox and one eye on the preacher, waiting for the ceremony. Reynard was gone, and the wedding proceeded without further interuption.

The Long-Bowled Pipe

Fox hunters were capable of various kinds of pranks, but nothing too far out. The kind of "fun" in which Watson indulged himself may be illustrated by the story of the long-bowled, corncob pipe Ed purchased during one of his numerous travels. He was certain that none of his foxhunting friends had seen this kind of pipe that appeared to hold an outlandish amount of tobacco.

The dogs had been released. The men gathered around the burning campfire, ready to listen to the dogs and exchange "pleasantries." As usual, they passed the bottle and pulled out their pipes for a smoke. All had brought out their pipes except the Colonel who was putting on quite an act, searching his pockets for his sack of Bull Durham.

Finally the men noted Watson's difficulty in finding his tobacco, and one of them proffered his sack. The stage had been set and it was then that the Colonel produced his false-bottomed, long-bowled pipe, with the comment that he "hated to take a man's entire sack."

The pipe always got the attention of the men and provided entertainment any time there was a new man on the hunt.

Picnic at Brushwood Lake

Around the campfire of a fox hunt south of town, Ed told about Dr. Woodson Moss, who was supposed to be chaperoning the junior and senior medical students on a picnic to Brushwood

51

Lake,* near the Katy tracks north of McBaine.

The edibles were stored in a large hamper and Dr. Moss was to sleep nearby, "just in case shenanigans were pulled." But next morning arrived and the edibles were gone. Someone then remembered hearing a lusty Missouri University yell as the Katy train crossed the bridge over the lake sometime during the night, and Dr. Moss recalled seeing two boys slide down a steep bank of Perche Creek about the time of the arrival of the picnic party.

By that time it finally dawned upon the juniors and seniors that the sophomores had stolen a march on them and had perpetrated a very practical joke. The hamper had been large and bulky and it had required considerable effort to carry it from the lake to McBaine, where the boys caught the Columbia-bound train, loaded the hamper aboard, and gave out their exultant shout as they passed over Brushwood Lake bridge.

In the late 1800's and early 1900's Watson and his friends rode horse-back on their fox hunts, but in the early 1920's the use of automobiles became general and although Ed could not drive, he always owned one of the cheaper-made cars. His favorite, a late 20's black Chevrolet van, easily transported his dogs. Watson had little difficulty locating a driver. One young fellow, a student in the University, and single, did practically all of his driving between 1927 and 1935, two years before Watson's death.

Rex McDonald the Greatest

On these hunts, even though horses were relegated to second place in transportation, they were the favorite subject of Watson when the dogs were not on the trail. Rex McDonald was his all-time favorite, appropriately so since Rex was the all-time world champion, the king of saddle stallions, and his home was in Columbia in the early 1900's. Rex sired many famous colts while in Columbia, including Star McDonald, which brought $2,500, and Grand McDonald, a fine, young stallion, the pride

52

Rex McDonald, the world's greatest 5-gaited stallion, born in neighboring Callaway County, was owned for a period of several years by a company in Columbia, headed by Dr. R.E. Graham, shown in the picture.

Ed Watson at his desk near the front door of the *Tribune,* then located at the corner of South Ninth and Locust streets. The typewriter in the foreground was used by long-time associate Hollis Edwards. The Duplex press is in the background.

of Paris, Mo., for which an offer of $3,000 was turned down. Watson was also a devotee of the race track. He travelled most frequently to New York tracks and the Kentucky Derby. He always pointed out to his listeners that Rex McDonald, when owned a short time in Kentucky by Col. Hughes, sired speed, and this was known only to a few people. J.B., a chestnut gelding offspring showed both speed and stamina in his races as a pacer at Wilkesbarre, Pa., and at other tracks in New York and Alabama.

Ed, willingly and with energy, entered into the controversy over Rex McDonald's birthplace:

> *There is a controversy going on among the newspapers of Audrain and Monroe counties as to where lies the native heath of that premier saddle stallion, Rex McDonald.*
>
> *It is pretty well established that Rex's dam was owned in Audrain and his sire in Callaway. Boone County doesn't care especially where he was bred in view of the fact that he is one of several great stallions that are owned here.*

He then explained that Rex McDonald was sired by Rex Denmark, Callaway-owned stallion; and the dam, Lucy Mack, had been sired by an Audrain-owned stallion, Black Squirrel. Joe McDonald of near Auxvasse, was given the credit for the mating of these fine animals.

Dr. R.E. Graham was president of the Rex McDonald Company. When he died the owners of the stallion sold the horse to Ben Middleton of Mexico. Mrs. Graham decided to take her young daughter back East to live and she called Middleton to bring Rex to the Wabash depot in Mexico for a farewell to the horse. Both the mother and the daughter were very fond of Rex, which returned their affection. About a year later, the great saddler died at the age of twenty-three years, the world's champion five-gaited saddle stallion, so great that he was ruled out of the competition in his middle years to give other horses a chance.

High Society and Diapers

As mentioned, Watson made many trips to the tracks. He enjoyed watching a horse race about as much as he liked a fox chase. On one occasion he had just returned from the famous Saratoga track in New York. His mother was helping him unpack, picking out his dirty shirts to send to the laundry. She ran across some four-cornered pieces of cloth that she recognized immediately.

"Ed," she said, "what are you doing with all these diapers?" Ed was as shocked as was she and he asked, "Are you sure those are diapers? I thought they were big handkerchiefs. As I was going out to the races, I bought these to put around my neck because the weather was hot. Here I was out there in all that big society with those darn diapers around my neck."

Forest King Lives in Style

Some of the famous local horses, other than Rex McDonald, were Forest King, Charles Reade and Columbia Girl. These horses showed in the Boone County Fair Horse Show of 1906. Forest King enjoyed more than the comforts of home, provided by his owner, Dr. William C. Gadsby. The box stall in which he lived was lined with green cloth and on the walls were a number of rugs of different colors. Rosa Bonheur's "Horse Fair" painting also adorned the walls, along with pictures of famous equine winners of the nation. A large mirror hung at one end of the stall. Forest King was undoubtedly pleased with his reflection, even though he occasionally trimmed back his ears and took a nip at the glass. The floor was covered with bright yellow straw which added to the colorings and appointments of the stall.

Forest King and his keeper, Frank Long, developed a deep attachment. Forest's stall was located at the stable of Shields & Courts. In order to guard against injury to the valuable stallion, Long slept in the same stall. It was said that the King would not lie down until his keeper came in to retire for the night. When bed-time came, the horse displayed uneasiness, walking rapidly back and forth in his stall, and stamping loudly. If Long was late in arriving, he voiced his displeasure by neighing. When Long appeared at the stall for the night, the horse demonstrated his pleasure by whinnying and rubbing his nose on his keeper's shoulder. Today Forest King's monument is standing near that of Stonewall King at the Boone County Fairgrounds.

During those years a very fine blood-bay gelding was owned by Columbian Alexander Bradford. Scotch High Ball had taken several first awards in the Worlds Fair Horse Show in St. Louis. He was by Charles Reed, a stallion of closer kin to Black Hawk, the progenitor of the Morgan strain, than any horse of that day.

Joe Folk, fine stallion named for Governor Folk, was sired by Forest Squirrel. Silver Bangles, the dam of Belle of Memphis and Johnnie McHale, was one of the best matrons in the county. She was owned by Dr. A.W. McAlester. Rex Denmark, Columbia-owned, and Chief Denmark of Howard County, were fine horses. Limestone Bell, the champion high school horse of Missouri and neighboring states, foaled a colt to Rex McDonald. It was a promising colt, but one that would never be a favorite of the ladies as was Bell, with her delightfully graceful execution and dainty ways. Her bow out of the ring at the close of an event and her high Spanish trot, at which she probably was never excelled by any high school performer always won her rounds of applause.

How to Train a Colt

Ed's interest in horses carried over into the bright and explicit imagery of his writing, frequently becoming an expression of his pilosophy. He encouraged farmers to practice the same

55

system of training with their colts that they used with their children, maintaining that this would make for fewer badly trained horses:

> *As soon as foaled, is the time to begin with the colt. We do not wait until they are nearly grown before we begin training our children, but they are taught a little every day. The same process will work out with the colt. Put a halter on it and teach it to lead; handle it gently and often, and when it is old enough to work, there will be less use for breaking carts and all the various appliances. "Breaking" the colt is indeed the proper term for many of them are "broken," so far as their future usefulness is concerned.*

Today's Business

Everyday life in the *Tribune* family was far from being dull. Ed Watson's good humor contributed to an atmosphere of congeniality at the office. There were always visitors, some with news stories or ads, and some just dropping by for a chat. One of the latter, Sid Rollins, chided Ed about the stacked papers and envelopes overflowing his desk. Unperturbed, Ed replied; "Mr. Rollins, that's just today's business."

* * *

The Prize Was $50,000

"Today's business" was a many-faceted operation. Pranks and practical jokes occasionally could be considered a by-product of the day's business. The "Boss" was capable of "having his fun," but he reserved the usual practice of it for his fox-hunting friends. Unwittingly, he was a part of a prank played at the office on Berkley Johnson, *Tribune* pressman. Berkley had entered a contest that had been advertised in the newspaper, and he was positive that he would win the $50,000 first prize. He was so sure of it that his fellow workers decided they would have some fun.

One of the reporters who worked on sports stories with telegrapher Barney Ward obtained a blank telegraph form from him and typed a message addressed to "Mr. Berkley Johnson." The message apprised Mr. Johnson that he was the winner of $50,000. Highly elated, Berkley took the telegram to Mr. Watson, shouting "I am rich, I am rich." Watson looked at the tele-

57

gram, perceived it to be phony, and tried to calm Berkley, not telling him that he thought the telegram was a fake, but that he thought it would be best to wait for more information, that it might not be as true as it seemed, that maybe he won only part of $50,000, that maybe it would be only a few dollars. Berkley finally calmed down and agreed that he would wait. Then he began to suspect that he was the victim of a prank, and he retreated to the pressroom with nothing more to say. He was morose for the rest of the day, but his usually good disposition reasserted itself the following day.

* * *

The Pig Story

In the early days of the *Tribune,* today's business included keeping an eagle eye out for success stories. Ed continuously sought stories from those people who had successfully sold items through the newspaper's classified ads, or who had found the ads useful in other ways.

One such "success story" he was fond of relating was his "pig story." One of Hartley Bank's pigs had strayed and Banks sought Ed Watson's help in recovering it by inserting a paid ad. Very shortly the pig returned home, "perhaps," according to Ed, "because he was a smart pig and read the Tribune's classified ads." When the pig returned to his stye, he brought with him a companion, "which indicated," said Ed, "why he left home in the first place."

This turn of events meant that Mr. Banks felt compelled to insert another ad, to discover what other unfortunate had lost a pig. On the day following publication of the ad, Alf Rees, a fox-hunting friend of Ed's, came in to inquire about the second lost pig ad, and was told to see Mr. Banks.

Ed said he was able to collect on only one of the ads, but

that he recovered his costs somewhat by the "success story" he ran on the day following Alf's recovery of his pig.

The Possum Story

Ed also had his "possum story," and this one involved another banker, R.B. Price Sr., and his hen house, where a big fat sassy possum was discovered. "For some time," Ed said, "Mr. Price's hens had been getting scarcer and scarcer, and the vigilance of the Price servitors had been increasing." Just as supper was served, a big commotion was heard in the henhouse.

John Fisher, an employee and one of the watchers, took his shotgun and hurried down to the hen house to shoot the chicken thieves. Instead of two-legged thieves, he found Mr. Possum curled up in a hen's nest, "playing possum." Fisher picked him up by the scruff of the neck and carried his prize to the house in state.

Col. Price, at the time president of the Boone County Possum Eaters Association, admitted that the possum would be "used." He could not decide, he said, "whether the possum, recognizing that his fate was settled, determined to come in and surrender at once, or whether he is the first of a series of possums who will pay my hen house a call on general principles."

* * *

In the Mood for Talking

Today's business was sometimes family business. The *Tribune* was family, and when Ed wanted to talk, he sought out members of his newspaper family. On one occasion, he was in the washroom and heard footsteps outside the door. He was ready to talk, and he called out, but received no answer. The footsteps were those of Bob Vickery, *Tribune* linotype operator, who at that particular moment, was not in the mood for talking. He turned and hurried back up front to his linotype, with Watson following not too far behind, but still out of sight. Bob occupied himself cleaning his machine, and Watson could see that he was quite busy, so he concluded that the footsteps had not been Bob's.

The only other person in the building was a high school student employed by the *Tribune* as mailer. He was doing some mailing room work and Watson decided that here was his culprit. He took the astonished young man by the ear and marched him to the washroom, saying as he went, that he did not like to be ignored. The young man was completely surprised by this precipitous action but could no nothing other than go to the washroom where the Boss regaled him on many subjects.

* * *

Just a Little Joke

When going to the washroom, "Watson always had a habit of kicking something—boxes, end rolls, or anything else that happened to be in his way as he went from his front desk to the rear of the building. The composing room employees knew this habit to be a part of everyday's business. One day several employees planned a surprise for the Boss. They filled a small box with linotype slugs, and placed it in his usual path to the washroom. Very shortly, he came along and gave the box a healthy kick. Out came the lead, and in ducked the heads of the perpetrators of the "little joke." Everybody concentrated on his work and the Boss continued on his way to the washroom. He also continued to kick things out of his way, but it was noted that his kicks had become less forceful.

* * *

Cash on Auction Sales

Edwin Moss Watson, the "Proprietor," believed in collecting whatever was due him. On one occasion, a local restaurant owed him some money that he had been unable to collect. He went to the restaurant, took in as payment a number of plates— all that he could carry—lugged them back to the *Tribune* office and passed them out to the *Tribune* family.

Political ads and auction sales were the prime losers of money for the newspaper. Politicians who won their elections paid up, but the losers usually had run out of money and, conveniently for them, but inconveniently for the *Tribune,* forgot to pay their bills. Those who held auctions were also bad risks. They sold out, and presumably left town. Anyway, the newspaper was left holding the bag. Watson decided to require cash on all auction sales. His reason for not including the politicians in the cash-required category, may be that they were all Democrats, and perhaps that was reason enough for Ed.

After employees were instructed on the new cash-for-sale-ad-policy, the first customer to bring in an ad was C.C. Bowling, prominent local banker. The girl at the front counter followed Mr. Watson's instructions and told Bowling that the transaction would have to be cash, a "new policy." This did not set well with Bowling who on many occasions had made accommodating loans to Watson. He got red in the face, said nothing, and walked out. Business Manager Jett was told of the incident by the counter girl and decided to talk to Jack Waters, the newspaper's advertising manager and Ed's nephew.* Jack hurried to the bank and arrived at the front door just as Bowling walked in. Jack assured Bowling that the policy did not apply to regular customers, that his credit was good, and that the ad would be taken back to the office for insertion in the paper. For awhile this ended the cash-in-advance-for-sale-ads.

* * *

Good Judge of Character

As with any newspaper, money was a part of the day's business. Business Manager Jett considered it the most important part of his day's business. A University student, who earned money as one of Jett's carriers, had become an habitual crapshooter. The young man, whom we will give the name of Hearne,* was sometimes lucky and sometimes not so lucky. He got behind with his paper bill and, with graduation time coming, Jett began to worry that the young man would not be able to pay his bill. Graduation day arrived and the bill was unpaid. Hearne promised Jett he would pay some day, but he said there was no possibility of paying before leaving town. Jett took the matter to the Boss, who said: "That's all right, I know Mr. Hearne and he'll be back some day and pay his bill."

Several years later, Hearne came in from California and paid the bill in full. Jett said he was surprised, but should have realized that the Boss was a good judge of character and was right as usual.

* * *

Office Mysteries

Odd and mysterious things can, and do, happen at any newspaper plant, but the "Mystery of the Missing Paste" in the early days of the *Tribune* was finally solved. The paste bucket, used in filling the paste magazine on the Duplex press, had been found empty each morning, despite the fact that it had been left half-full at night. The editorial staff was accused by the linotype operator of using a quart of paste a day in preparing "reprint copy" from other papers, but this was vigorously denied by the scissors and paste people.

One morning, Carl Schwamb, foreman of the composing room, started to reach into the paste barrel to scoop up enough paste to replenish the editorial paste pot, and discovered the paste-eating culprits. Seven rats, large and small, tried to climb his arm toward freedom. Carl jerked back and quickly clapped a board cover over the barrel, making the rats "captives of war." In due time, the rats were let out, one at a time, in front of a rat dog, and their life history closed.

Less than a year later, another mystery unravelled when a friendship bracelet, which had been brought to the *Tribune* by the finder for the purpose of locating the owner, was missing again. It had vanished from the cash drawer, and the *"Tribune,"** that is, Ed Watson, was unable to produce the bracelet, for its owner. This was a source of considerable embarrassment to Watson, and when remnants of it were found in another desk— in a drawer of the business manager's desk—it proved to be a double embarrassment. The conclusion was soon drawn, however, that a hungry mouse had carried it from one desk to the other where it had eaten the leather strap. The links and the metal buckle were undamaged, and were made available to the owner.

* * *

Buggies for Babies

Not every day were new little members added to the *Tribune* family, but when they were, it was the Boss' practice to buy fancy baby buggies for the new arrivals. The buggies were fine looking and the mothers, on their first out-of-the-house visit, proudly paraded their new-born offspring down to the *Tribune* office to see Mr. Watson at his desk. Buggy owners included Mr. and Mrs. M.D. Jett, Mr. and Mrs. Mike C. Creasy, Mr. and Mrs. Clyde Hopper, with twin girls, Mr. and Mrs. Carl Schwamb, and others.

* * *

Chickens in the Basement

The Day's Business many times was not a cash business. Chickens and other produce were frequently taken in exchange for subscriptions, and were stored temporarily in the basement of the *Tribune*, where the Rev. R.S. "Parson" Cunningham, a good printer and a part-time preacher, leased space for his job printing shop. Some of the chickens disappeared, and Watson, knowing that Parson's temper could be ruffled, asked him if he knew where the chickens were? Parson wasn't happy at all with the question.

Just at that time, Edwin Moss, who had heard part of the converstion between Watson and Parson, came down the basement steps. Parson was red-faced, and with tobacco juice running down one side of his mouth onto his chin, he spluttered to Moss: "Imagine anyone accusing a man of God with stealing chickens." Moss knew then that Mr. Watson had succeeded in having fun and getting his "rise" out of his old friend.

* * *

Off-Color Schemes

Sometimes the day's business included crooks. Ed Watson was an honest man—unapproachable on a scheme that was offbeat. He refused ads that appeared dishonest to him. He sometimes chased out of the office those who had presented off-color schemes. He did not care how prominent the person might be—it could be the Mayor of Columbia—it made no difference. He still raised hell with the proponent of the doubtful scheme.

People were always embarrassed at his forthright outbursts. Whenever he said, in a loud voice, "Get out of here," he meant it. His reaction to something not legitimate was violent, and this violence was demonstrated on more than one occasion.

Likewise he never allowed salesmen to pester him. If they

pressed him to buy something, he could get upset. One such salesman asked him: "Why don't you buy it?" The response was: "Because I don't want to, that's why...now get out."

Most of the time he was courteous and kind and gentle. People who were readers of his sometimes violent editorials were always surprised, upon meeting him, at his gentility. He was especially courteous to women, and never would you hear him raise his voice to a woman. This might have meant that women did not present to him off-color schemes. But, more than likely, it could be explained by the fact that Ed Watson was reared in the old Southern tradition of respect for womanhood.

An instance of his regard for women occurred one morning when he was particularly incensed at a political shyster who had dropped by the office for a visit. Betty Badgerow, the classified advertising girl, was the only young lady who happened to be in the office at the time, and Watson sent her home, telling her that he "wanted to use a few choice words that he did not think she should hear." Betty went home and someone else did her work that day.

Backed His Employees

Queen Smith, another lady employee, was society editor of the *Tribune* for many years. She tells a story about the man from near McBaine in southern Boone County, who came in to complain about a mistake in the paper. She was in the process of explaining that the error was hers, and that she was "very sorry." At this point when she was about to placate the man, Watson came up out of his chair, storming, and telling the man that Queen did not make the mistake.

"Mr. Watson was unpredictable," Queen said, "but I knew he was always on my side. His taking up for me was appreciated but it did make my problem with the man from South county a little more difficult."

Have You Visited Smokey?

Watson's friends could be found in every walk of life. Those who were his fox hunting friends were tall and short, fat and thin, educated and uneducated. His relationship with people of all shades of belief, of all scales of the social ladder, is demonstrated by his friendship with the bootblack at the Tiger Barber Shop.

Friend Smokey was not doing too well financially with his shoe-shining business, and Watson thought he had the answer. He would run an ad for Smokey for six days. The first ad in the February 13, 1906 issue of the *Tribune*, was as follows:

HAVE YOU VISITED SMOKEY

The old and original Smokey is at the Tiger Barber Shop, and will be found there any time you need him. He is well-known throughout the country. He is a bootblack with reference; slow but sure at all times. If you need any work done in his line of business he will be glad to have you phone or call him at the Tiger Barber Shop, 908 Broadway. Yours truly, A. Customer.

"A. Customer" was Ed Watson. Eight days later he decided to put to use his propensity for versifying and wrote the following:

Where I shine,
Waiting on you is my delight;
I will shine your shoes,
And shine them right.

Those who have tried me
Certainly know
That I shine the heel
As well as the toe.

When you're at leisure
I'll be glad to have you stop
Where I shine 'em up
In the Tiger Barber Shop.

Smokey

Colonel Watson in his dress uniform as a member of Governor Guy B. Park's Honorary Colonel's staff. He is standing at the front door of the Belvedere Apartments on Hitt Street, where he lived following the death of his mother.

A Broadway scene of the 1920's, looking northeast, with the Broadway Methodist Church at the corner of Short Street and Broadway in the background. Note cars parked in middle of street.

This was signed "Smokey," but Smokey had been given help by a man who spent a lot of time helping people who needed help.

* * *

Meeting the Trains

Watson also offered help to his nephew Jack Waters. During high school summers, Jack had "met the trains" for the *Tribune*. When he came back to Columbia in 1918, following service at Ft. Sheridan during World War I, his Uncle Ed again offered him a job as part-time reporter, but Jack had plans to follow in the footsteps of his grandfather, Dr. B.A. Watson, in pursuit of the medical profession. After a year and a half, he changed his major and then accepted the reportorial job from his Uncle. After graduation in 1923, he became a reporter on a Kansas City newspaper for a few months. Upon returning to Columbia in 1924, he accepted his Uncle's offer of a combination job, that of reporter and advertising manager.

Uncle Ed, always ready to help his nephew, offered to support Jack if he wanted to enter politics, but again Jack had other plans and turned down the offer. Jack's father, by then past-president of Kansas State University, had been interested in national politics, and was considered by President Woodrow Wilson for a post in his cabinet as Secretary of Agriculture. However, a no-name was selected for the post, and Dr. Waters dropped out of the national picture. He was still a potent force in the midwest, and became editor of the *Kansas City Weekly Star* in 1917, which post he held until his death in 1925.

Calming a Volcano

"Uncle Ed had a soft spot in his heart for nephew Jack," according to Bob Vickery. "Jack could work with his uncle when anyone else would have had trouble," said Vickery. "It was like

67

calming a volcano, but Jack had the patience to stay with him."

When Vickery first went to work for the *Tribune*, he was just beginning his studies in the Journalism School, going to classes in daytime and working nights at the *Tribune* as a linotype operator. Watson, as a bachelor with time on his hands, spent many late night hours at the office. Frequently he took over Bob's evening working hours, talking about many subjects, but mostly discussing one of his favorite topics, the breeding lines of horses. "He knew them all," said Bob, "from Rex McDonald back to his Black Squirrel and Denmark ancestry."

When Mike Creasy, composing room foreman, arrived on the following morning, he found only two or three hours work accomplished by Bob, when there should have been five or six hours work completed. The pay, according to Mike, was to be given at the end of the week for the two or three hours, and there was nothing Bob could do. Watson wanted someone to talk to, and Bob was chosen. Even though Mike knew the problem, he was a stickler for paying only for a job's actual work. All this was unknown to Watson, of course. "In Mike's favor," said Bob, "when the Tribune strike was called off, and I was the new Foreman, Mike worked for me, but did not complain or hold a grudge against me for superseding him as Foreman."

During a period of seven years, from 1931 to 1937, Vickery handled the typesetting of all of the Boss' editorials. This "honor" was his because Watson discovered that Bob could read his scribble. Even so, there were times when even Bob found that he could not translate a particularly difficult scrawl. "On these occasions," said Bob, "it so happened that whenever I could not translate, neither could Mr. Watson." Then the two of them worked over the paragraph, and rewrote it so that it made sense. "Never once did he show impatience with me for my inability to read his writing." Bob said.

Watson usually wrote his editorials in the morning for the afternoon paper. He always used a large Samuel Bingham pencil with soft lead and a big eraser, obtained for him by business manager Jett. Newspaper supply salesmen who made regular calls on the *Tribune,* brought the pencils along as a special favor to Jett. Of typewriters, Watson said: "I never became reconciled to the contraptions." But his associate, City Editor Hollis Edwards, could make a typewriter rattle with a two-fingered hunt and peck system.

* * *

Hiring a Reporter

Another employee, Clyde H. Duncan, for many years with the *Arkansas Farmer,* published in Little Rock, told of his first introduction to Ed Watson: "I was awakened about midnight by a knock at my door at the Y.M.C.A. I jumped to my feet, unlocked the door, and met for the first time, Col. Ed Watson. That was in early September, 1924 and marked the opening of a new world for me, challenging days on the *Columbia Daily Tribune.*

"Col. Ed, as so many people knew him, was living at the Daniel Boone Tavern, and sometimes he would take a stroll around the down-town area. On this evening as he passed the Y.M.C.A., he recalled that a student lived there whom he wanted to see, to discuss the matter of a reporting job, specifically the daily coverage of the University news beat.

"My name had come to him by way of his friend, Dr. W.C. Etheridge, long-time head of the University's Field Crops Department, and an active participant with Col. Ed in shaping the policies of the then nearly defunct Democratic Party, whose opposition was headed at the national level by a stern-faced Vermonter, by the name of Calvin Coolidge. These two—Ed Watson and W.C. Etheridge—held many a talk-fest over the remaking of the world in general, and the ousting of Coolidgeites in particular. Their gabfests were usually held after press-time at the *Tribune.*

"That night in 1924 when Col. Ed roused me from my rest, he was, as always, the very soul of gentility and warmth. He apologized for appearing at my door at such a late hour, but his apologies, couched in Elizabethan prose, came naturally and were certainly acceptable. I was then in my junior year at the University College of Agriculture, and had been the second student enrolled in the new course in Agricultural Journalism.

"Col. Ed came to the point of his visit soon after his explanation for being up at that hour. It seems the Elks had held a very late initiation, and he had, as he said, 'imbibed a bit too heavily of the herbs, and was just out indulging the night air to wear off the aroma so long associated with the viands of the gods.' In short, he told me he wanted me to come by the *Tribune* the next day and start covering the University beat. As he tucked his cane under his arm, and started down the steps to the Y.M.C.A. lobby, he called over his shoulder: 'How would fifteen a week suit you?'

"I could hardly sleep all that night. Now I could get a lot of practical experience, and at the same time attend the University, and eat three square meals a day. The 'Greasy Spoon,' as students affectionately called a restaurant operated by the Morris brothers from Centralia, made it possible to eat high on the hog for a dollar a day. Since my room at the Y.M.C.A. cost only $2.50 a week, I was truly in 'high cotton,' to use an Arkansas expression. The next morning I reported to the news editor of the *Tribune,* Hollis Edwards.

"At the time I was taking a five-hour course in Small Town Newspaper Reporting. It consisted mostly in reporting to the basement offices of the *Herald-Statesman* on South Ninth Street for practical writing assignments from Prof. John H. Casey. In that class was one, Joe Simpich, who was the darling of the campus for several reasons. Joe was a World War I hero, and a popular student government officer of some kind or other. I think Joe was vice-president, and Rusty Casteel was the student

70

president. At any rate Joe was a very popular student, and his prestige was further enhanced by the fact that he had a brother who was on the editorial staff of the *National Geographic*. Joe seemed to think that with such a pedigree, which stretched from the Argonne, Belleau Woods and back again, he had free leeway never to darken a University classroom. He seldom did, and seldom did I, especially in that course. I felt I was getting about all the reporting I needed on the *Tribune*.

"Prof. Casey one day noted that Joe Simpich and Clyde Duncan had hardly attended any class periods that semester. So, he blandly announced, within earshot of everyone, that the next issue of the *Herald-Statesman* would be put out in its entirety by Messers. Simpich and Duncan.

"At the class' end, amid stares from class members, I walked across the street to the *Tribune* office, prepared to lay my problem squarely in the lap of the Boss, Ed Watson. It was close to press-time, and he was hurriedly proof-reading his editorial for the day. He waved me aside in his gentle way, and said as soon as he had finished he would give my problem his immediate attention."

One of Our Number in Trouble

"In a few minutes he had finished with the editorial, and when I related my problem about the possibility of an F grade, he said: 'You and Joe will be a bit short-handed, also probably a bit lonely,' he smiled. Then he called Hollis to his desk and told him to 'regroup the troops,' to get ready to send every person on the *Tribune* including Sports Editor Jake Hamel and others, over to the *Herald-Statesman* for one night's work. He added, 'One of our number is in trouble, and we must stick together.'

"At the next class period I was able to lay in Prof. Casey's hands the complete issue of the *Herald-Statesman*. As the Professor turned the pages, and read the editorials, he said: 'Seems I can detect a lot of the *Tribune* in this paper.' Finally, with a smile, he came to the paper's last page, and looking at Joe and me, he said: 'Well you two have surprised me very much. You both have passed the course with a grade of 'E.' As we left the classroom, Joe said to me: 'You and the *Tribune* staff bailed me out this time, but don't forget, I bailed all of you out in the Argonne.' And he, and others like him, had."

"My fondest memories are my last two days in Columbia, Col. Ed surprised me with a banquet at Charley McAlester's cafeteria, down the street from the *Tribune*. Next morning, before the noon Wabash arrived, the Y.M.C.A. band paraded ahead of me, and student friends rolled me and my suitcase down Broadway in a wheel-barrow to the station. Col. Ed had arranged for this last minute bit of fun and frolic to make sure that I knew full well that my months as a *Tribune* staffer had been appreciated."

* * *

In Kind of a Hurry

Another employee of Watson's was Hamilton "Ham" Johnson, who started working for Ed Watson while still in high school in the 1920's.

"I did flat-casting and ran the old flat-bed press, helping Johnny Sullivan," said Ham. "Then Johnny went with the *Missourian* and I became head pressman. In 1927 we bought the tubular press and I got Berkley Johnson, my cousin, to help me. It took two people to run the tubular, 8-page press, because one man had to man the rolls and the other the folder end of the press. Later we added another eight pages, giving us sixteen pages.

"One experience I had with Mr. Watson was the time I forgot to put the center pieces back in, after taking them out for a center spread. Gradually after picking up speed, the lead plates broke into pieces and flew here and there over-head—a very dangerous situation, but fortunately no one was in the path of the pieces of broken lead. A cylinder was sprung and could no longer be used.

"I went up to talk to Mr. Watson, telling him that I was in kind of a hurry and forgot to put the center pieces in, busting the cylinder.

"He said: 'Don't they make cylinders every day? Can't you get a new one?' I told him yes, but they were expensive, about $900. He had Mr. Jett call Chicago or New York, got a press erector worker in with the cylinder and we were using the full sixteen pages very shortly. In the menantime we used twelve pages."

* * *

Called Them Mister

Many *Tribune* carriers moved on to good positions in later life. Most of them "worked their way through the University" and were happy to have work at the newspaper. Watson was interested in his working carriers and he knew them all by name. Most of them, however, he called "Mister" even though he knew their first names.

One of his carriers was Edwin Moss, who started delivering papers when the *Tribune* was located at 23 North Ninth Street. The office was in what was called the Nowell Annex, next door to the Nowell Grocery, then located at the corner of Ninth and Walnut streets. Moss remembered when the *Tribune* had under 2,000 subscribers and he delivered 200 of them in the southeast part of town. He also recalled that Mr. Watson was "quite affable" and that he always dignified Edwin by calling him "Mister Moss." Years later, Moss was a pressman for the *Tribune.*

When Moss began carrying papers in 1919, Mr. Watson was on a trip to Canada, but Edwin had been hired before he left. Moss was hired, presumably, because both he and the Boss had come from the Millersburg area and both had the names "Edwin Moss."

"Mr. Watson was visiting the paper mills in Canada and his visit extended close to Christmas," Moss said. "He must have been homesick, and he wanted to do something at Christmas time for his carriers. He sent back Five Dollar gold pieces, which was a lot of money in those days.

"My gold came in handy," continued Moss, "my family was hard up, having just come from the farm to town, with no one, outside of myself, working. That gold piece was exchanged for coal to heat our house."

* * *

Another carrier, Jack Bell, who worked his way through Journalism School peddling Tribunes, was sized up by Watson: "Mister Bell is a bright and brash young man who will go far." Later, Bell became nationally famous as a correspondent for the Associated Press in Washington, D.C.

* * *

Print It Kindly

Wendell H. Crow, who left a CCC camp in Arkansas in 1934 to work for Ed, was a printer's devil in the back shop, and also carried papers for a time. When he left Columbia with a degree in journalism, plus extra graduate credit, he had imbibed much of Ed Watson's philosophy of newspapering.

"Colonel Ed filled me with awe," Crow said, "and I was aware of his human-kindness, even before I got into Jay* School. The four weeklies I've owned and edited carried much of him into other places, for I tried to follow what precepts I picked up from watching him, into my own editing. For instance his phrase 'We print the news but we print it kindly,' when someone objected to how the *Tribune* carried a story and demanded a retraction, which he refused to do (believing the story was accurate), I used many times when it happened to me under the same circumstances over the years."

* * *

Knives to Employees

Ed Watson was fond of making gifts to his employees. The season need not be Christmas time. The kinds of gifts made were unpredictable. It was no particular holiday, and for no particular reason, that Watson went to Newman Hardware Store, where he bought a dozen or so knives to give away to his employees. He also bought one for himself because he was unable to use a pencil sharpener on the big pencils he used for his editorial writing. But he lost his knife shortly after buying it, and from then on walked over to Monroe Jett's desk to borrow "our knife," as he called it.

This dual use of the knife continued for some time, but one day Watson came over to Jett's desk, expressing dismay: "I can't find 'our knife,' and I know I borrowed it." This was in the Fall. Spring came along and one day Watson walked in the front door beaming. "Mr. Jett, I found 'our knife,' and he held it up for Jett to see. "It was in my pants pocket last Fall, and this Spring when I pulled the pants out of the closet, I found it." He was as pleased as a small child over his find.

* * *

Dust Collector

When Ed Watson bought the *Tribune,* he had already enjoyed a wide acquaintanceship with University professors, from University of Missouri president, R.H. Jesse, down. The University was small, numbering less than 2,000 students, and the town of Columbia had a population of less than 5,000. When President Jesse gave Ed his favorite hat rack, it meant that the two were good friends, despite the gift. It was an Elk head with widely extended antlers, mounted on a formidable looking oak cabinet. Everybody called it a dust collector, and for many years it took up much space in a corner of the newsroom.

Silly Old Cow

Another professor, with whom Ed enjoyed friendship, was Dr. William Benjamin Smith, one of the world's great mathematicians. The professor was not only absent-minded but also so concentrated in his world of the intellect that he often forgot where he was going or had been.

One night quite late, as the Professor was returning home in the dark he stepped from the board walk down into the street, removed his hat and apologized to a Jersey cow that he chanced to encounter. Before he had gone another block, he was again lost in meditation, and again he bumped into something. This time he said: "Why don't you keep off the walk, you silly old cow!" And by the time the words were out of his mouth, he discovered that he was addressing a very charming young lady who lived just around the corner from his home, and who had been making a belated call on his wife.

So, far from being offended, the young lady thought the joke was altogether too good to keep, and she never failed to tell it when she and Dr. Smith were out in society. Ed also kept the story alive.

Rising above politics

Hugh Stephens, a friend of Ed's going back many years, was about to be dropped as a member of the State Highway Commission by Republican Governor Sam A. Baker. Ed heard

76

about the Governor's plans and wrote an editorial entitled: "Rising Above Politics." The editorial opposed Gov. Baker's possible changing of members of the State Highway Commission. He wrote: "The people of the state want no interference with the road commission that has given the state one of the best systems in the country."

The editorial appeared in the January 6, 1927 issue of the *Tribune,* and five days later, January 11, a news item in the *Tribune* stated that "Governor Baker changed his mind about dropping Stephens." Also, "Cutler was approved as Chief Engineer." Gov. Baker originally had wanted H.H. Lotter as his Chief Engineer.

* * *

St. Patrick was an Engineer

Ed Watson had many friends among train personnel on both the Katy and the Wabash. Conductors, brakemen and porters always knew him by name and he, in turn, knew them well enough to inquire about their families. The pullman porters took good care of his needs, and he enjoyed talking to them.

One of his railroad stories concerned a St. Patrick's Day incident. Ed was on a St. Louis-bound train that pulled into Union Station with large, green-painted posters plastered on the sides of the cars.

When he arrived in St. Louis he saw a big Irishman puzzling over the signs and carefully spelling out one: ST. PATRICK WAS AN ENGINEER. And then the Irishman gave a whoop and a shout. He understood that M.U. students of engineering at Columbia had painted the signs, but he did not understand why. When one of the passengers explained the meaning of the signs, he gave another shout and commented quite favorably of the "great school where they venerate St. Patrick."

* * *

Church Hymns

In his early days Ed Watson was a fairly regular church-goer at the First Baptist Church. He had two good examples in church-going, his mother and his boss, E.W. Stephens, who had taught Sunday School many years, and was a prominent leader in the Baptist Church, state-wide.

Not only was Ed a conservative church-goer, but also a conservative in his selection of church hymns. "I always feel doubtful," he said, "about the religion of the minister who gives out some new-fangled, unknown hymn for his congregation to stumble through. It results usually in a few moments of more or less mis-mated noise, and then a subsidence of all organized effort and fervor, as opposed to that with which everybody joins in on "All Hail the Power of Jesus' Name."

Watson was not a conservative when he opposed those in the church who railed against dancing. He and his sister, Stella, were dancing regulars at Stone's Music Hall* on South Ninth Street. Stella, who was two years older than Ed, always carried her dancing shoes in a fancy, silk bag, because walking in mud over stepping stones could be disastrous to dancing shoes. The dances were called "Balls," and the "June Balls" were held by fraternities and sororities each year. The kind of dance steps that were popular were waltzes and two-steps. Ed and Stella also entertained at home, with the latter playing the piano, and boarders contributing their voices. Many young folks gathered around the piano in those days.

* * *

Sunday Morning Loafers

When the subject of religion was discussed, Oler Hombs, a regular visitor to the *Tribune* office, saw eye to eye with Ed. One

Sunday morning the two friends were loafing at the newspaper office. Neither had gone to church that morning, and they were reviewing the Ten Commandments, which had been memorized by both men in their earlier years.

They started with the first commandment: I am the Lord Thy God; thou shalt not have strange gods before me. Ed commented that "this was the first and best because the fool has said in his heart: there is no God." "Well Ed," said Oler, "I guess we keep this commandment, but what about the next?" He recited; "Thou shalt not take the name of the Lord Thy God in vain. Now there's one, Ed, that I have to keep scrupulously when I'm around my wife." And Ed agreed that a woman's presence would cause one to be careful.

Ed took the next commandment: Remember that thou keep holy the Sabbath Day. "Oler," he said, "We're keeping it this morning, all right, but what's going to happen this afternoon?"

"The next commandment gives you no trouble," said Oler. "Honor thy Father and thy Mother comes easy enough for you."

Ed took the next one, Thou shalt not kill, and commented that "he had felt like killing, but had refrained."

Oler came to the next one, Thou shalt not commit adultery, and said, "I guess we'll pass that one by."

Ed agreed and quickly went to Thou shalt not steal. "No, Oler, I don't think I've ever stolen—except a watermelon or two."

Oler suggested that the next one, Thou shalt not bear false witness against thy neighbor, was the hardest of all of them, and both agreed it was more difficult to follow by far than the last which dealt with coveting your neighbor's wife and his property.

That was one Sunday morning that the Sunday loafers at the *Tribune* heard an ear-full. But they lost interest when the conversation turned to foxhounds and horses.

Big Hats in Church

None but a church-goer could write with such accuracy the editorial Ed titled BIG HATS AND SPIRITUALITY:

No one can attain spiritual exaltation sitting in church behind an exaggerated aggregation of straw, feathers and ribbons. Removing hats in churches is just as important as removing them at places of amusement. What degree of pleasure can an auditor get who hears a speaker and is not able to see his face? Possibly some, but it's the kind furnished by a phonograph. After a half hour of neck craning and side peeping in a vain attempt to see the preacher, wouldn't it be strange if part of the congregation, at least, comes away wishing they had stayed at home. Despite these inconveniences to other people, Christian women will wear the most exaggerated millinery conceits imaginable and calmly block the vision of three or four unfortunates behind them. It is a safe guess that the expressed thoughts of the victims would not sound well in a sanctuary.

It is a gratification that the edict from Paris is for small hats. It is hoped that every woman in the land will be stylish and up-to-date to a degree. Those who still cling to the megatherium type of head gear are implored in heaven's name to remove them in church and not jeopardize the soul's salvation of those behind them who are weak in the flesh.

Ed's respect for the dead went back to his earliest boyhood, and was inherited from his mother who instilled in him the idea of taking care of the family cemetery on the Hunt place. A few choice words in an editorial gives his feeling for drivers who break through funeral lines:

Barbarians have respect for the dead, but some Columbia residents have not. Several times lately, while funeral corteges have been moving toward the cemetery, drivers of vehicles have broken through the line regardless of everything but their own convenience. Such acts are worse than barbarous because those who commit them know better. No haste excuses the perpetrators. Common decency is wanting in such and they deserve the condemnation of every one. There is probably no way to reach the ilk above mentioned, but if there is it should be invoked.

The variety of Watson's viewpoints were scattered throughout his years in editorial and editorial notes, some of them in his Maverick notes. Below are some of them:

Isn't it strange what a splash of color even a blue jay makes against a gray tree trunk in winter—like a cheerful laugh on a gloomy day.

On respect he wrote:

What a fine thing respect for our elders is. If you see a young man who has a natural respect for old people or even those but a few years older than he, you can put it down there is much good in him. Students should always show a great deal of respect for their professors whether they like them or not. The old should always be reverenced. You who look at old people and think of the time when you will be old need little of this advice. This talk is only for the thoughtless, those who live for today. Respect is a noble thing, and it will not hurt anyone to possess considerable of it.

God and Humor

Ed Watson had a definite philosophy of life, well-expressed. He held a strong belief in a Supreme Being but never intruded it on his readers. His definition of humor was an expression of his everyday life, and was his answer to the local preacher who "wondered if God had a sense of humor." Ed commented: "That's the one thing God must have. Humor is everyday love."

Watson's thought for tomorrow: "It may never come." His philosophy of "doing good and laughing" was expressed in an editorial:

81

Christ directed us to "do unto others as ye would be done by," for human nature is built so that its natural and unconscious impulse is to "do unto others as ye are done by." That is why it pays to be good to your fellowman. He will pay it back. "Laugh and the world laughs with you," because it can't help it. Frown, and you'll be let alone.

A general disbelief in hell was beginning to be expressed in the press of the day on which Ed commented:

We believe a good many people are afraid of fire and that if preachers in general could in some manner slip a convincing idea of brimstone to their timid brethren, it might have a salutary effect.

The Old Time Religion

Not only were the editors of newspapers bitten with the virus of Modernism but preachers of the day were also succumbing to the virus:

Laymen seem to be satisfied with the old-time religion and the divinity of Christ, but the pastors, the shepherds of the people, the ones who are supposed to lead aright, are seemingly endeavoring in every way possible to discredit the Bible, Jesus Christ, and seemingly are in a fair way to reflect on God Almighty, Himself.

Watson's prediction that a war with Japan would come was expressed in an editorial note December 3, 1906:

Sooner or later Japan will wage war against the United States. After that the little yellow men will not want to fight for a long time to come.

On "Graft," he said:

We don't agree with "Checkers" who said: "Ain't it hell to be poor." We ordinary people out here in the little town of Columbia should not envy those who have better financial success in the world, some of them at least. Every day we read of grafting. We have been reading of it for years. There are apparently a million forms of grafting. Most of it is done by people who receive high salaries, men who are in positions of privilege. Yet we don't envy them. The grafters are the people who like to splurge, the high flyers that are always trying to live in the class above their means. You don't find the graft and grafters among the steady, satisfied, substantial people of the small cities and towns.

* * *

Boone County Hospital

The Boone County Hospital, an institution that received the full support of Ed Watson, was familiarly designated by him as the B.C. Hunt Place. And there was a reason for this. When the newly organized Kiwanis club decided in 1922 to build a gateway for the new hospital, B.C. Hunt, cashier of the Columbia Savings Bank, was serving as the Kiwanis club's first president. At the gateway to the hospital, on the posts at either side of the driveway were the initials B.C.H., which were supposed to stand for Boone County Hospital. Hunt always disclaimed any responsibility for the initials, but Ed Watson never let him forget about the coincidence.

Watson was a friend of the hospital through the years and was personally acquainted with all the physicians in Columbia, dating back to the days when his father was a prominent and respected physician of the city, among twenty-two other medical practitioners in a city of about 6,000 population.

Fried Chicken Night

Ed's personal physician in later years was Dr. G.A. Bradford, who lived only a block down the street from the *Tribune* office when it was at the corner of Ninth and Locust streets. A short distance east of Dr. Bradford's was the Belvedere Apartments on Hitt Street, where Watson lived. The good doctor had put Ed on a diet for high blood pressure and for excess weight. Ed was permitted, among other foods, baked not fried, chicken, and so it happened that on or about 3:00 o'clock one morning Ed Watson had gotten hungry. He called Dr. Bradford out of bed to ask him if it would be all right to eat some fried chicken. The Doctor wanted to know where he could get fried chicken, or any kind of chicken, at that hour of the morning, and was told that "Logan" had the chicken and was ready to fry it. The Doctor gave his permission without argument so that he could get back to bed.

Valuable Valet

Logan, whose full name was Logan Thompson, was a short, slightly built, black man, who rolled his overall legs half-way up to his knees, and walked with a side-to-side, rolling gate. This peculiar walk was said to have resulted from an injury sustained in World War I. He was a grandson of slaves owned in the 1860's by Dr. Watson's family. He performed many services for his Boss, including errands, cleaning the apartment, and cooking night-time snacks. With tongue in cheek, Watson called his loyal helper his "Valuable Valet."

Logan and the Boss got along in good fashion most of the time but occasionally there were unimportant mishaps that occurred. One such incident was leaked to the public when the Boss arrived one morning at the *Tribune* office complaining that he was having trouble with his false teeth. He mentioned this to several employees. He hadn't yet gone to Morris'* for his breakfast, and didn't know how troublesome the teeth might be. About the time he was ready to leave the office for the restaurant, his "Valuable Valet" walked in the front door, also complaining about the fit of his false teeth, and before any more of the public could be privy to their dilemma, Ed quickly took Logan to the washroom where they exchanged teeth.

* * *

84

Love of Children

Mention has been made of Clara Watson's love for children, a proclivity she passed on to Edwin. One of Ed's stories concerned the little lady from Paris, Mo., who was visiting her grandfather, George Ashlock, who incidentally, had married into the Ward clan. The little girl presented a "surprise from Santa Claus" to her grandfather who accepted it with thanks. Then he sat back in his chair, ostensibly to enjoy the pipe she had given him.

"But grandfather," she said, "Don't you know I expected you to surprise me too?" Grandfather was waiting for this and pulled out a big package. Then he "watched the little lady's eyes get bigger than the package."

Another of his stories concerned the five-year-old niece of Tom Ballew, who put her uncle on the spot. Little Helen Selby and her three-year-old younger brother, Watson, were the owners of several white turkeys. One of the turkeys was killed by a snake coiling around its neck, and Helen insisted on a regulation funeral—shroud, grave, coffin, preacher and all. When the funeral was all ready to proceed the little directoress said, "Now Uncle Tom, you pray." But Uncle Tom demurred, saying someone else should do it. The little girl insisted that it would be no funeral unless there was a prayer by Uncle Tom. "You pray, I'll sing, and Watson can cry," she offered. It is said that Uncle Tom fled precipitately rather than face the ordeal of improvising a prayer.

There was the story of another uncle who didn't need any prayers:

James H. Moss, of this city has recently been to Jefferson City, and made an excellent impression on his little niece, the 4-year-old daughter of Hugh Stephens, of that city. After Mr. Moss' visit, the little girl was saying her prayers, and she remembered many of her relatives, her father, mother, grandfather, grandmother and Uncle Jim—then she corrected herself by saying: "No, Uncle Jim is good; he does not need praying for."

Another little Miss, 6-year-old Dorothy Briggs, who visited Columbia in November, 1909, had been born in the Philippine

85

Islands, where her father, Prof. George Briggs, was director of a trade school in Manila. Ed decided that he would interview the little globe-trotter for the *Tribune.* His first question was: "Were you born in the Philippines?" And she nodded assent. "Are you a Filipino?" With this important question, Miss Briggs drew herself up in a very dignified manner and said: "No, I am not either."

Curfew for Nighthawks

During Watson's first year as owner of the *Tribune,* he was troubled by the fact that so many youngsters of the town were getting into difficulty with the law. His first editorial on the subject called for a curfew:

If the parents of these little nighthawks will not, or cannot, keep them off the street, a city ordinance and the police should be invoked to assist them. The council should get busy with a curfew ordinance. Boys between ten and sixteen years roam the streets every night without restraint. A curfew bell or whistle would stop all this and would check the downward tendencies of some of the young Bedouins.

Ed had seen a small boy of nine years sent to the reform school at Boonville. He saw a mother ask the court to put her 13-year-old daughter in "safe-keeping" at the women's reformatory at Chillicothe. He had seen many children running around late at night and getting into trouble, and had pushed for a curfew ordinance until the city council finally passed one "to get Ed Watson off our back." The council arranged with E.W. Stephens for his publishing company whistle to be blown each night at 9 o'clock.

Watson knew where tramps and loafers came from, and he compared the life of a small boy who was turned loose, to that of a Ten Dollar pup that was not turned loose. In one of his editorial notes he wrote:

*If a man has a Ten Dollar pup he will look after it careful-
ly and not let it run all over town, but if he has a boy, it
may be different. He is turned loose at a certain age and
let go to the devil. The people wonder where the great
army of tramps, loafers, dead beats and sots come from
in each decade. They are germinated from pure seed,
gathered from homes and sown broadcast upon our
streets and alleys. It may be your boy is starting in that
direction. At all events the boy ought be be given the
same chance with the pup.*

Watermelon Poaching is Risky

Considered a "softy" in his relationships with children, Ed
wrote about the boys from Rocky Fork neighborhood who were
caught poaching watermelons, and were brought into town,
where they were fined $1 each. He commented editorially:

*If there is any crime that ought to be excused, it is that of
the small boy who carried away the watermelon. All of
you have vivid recollections of standing near a watermelon patch with your boyish companions and looking upon
the hundreds of fat melons basking in the sun. You were
hungry and the farmer had so many of them; surely he
wouldn't care if a couple of them were swiped. You remember you talked about getting shot with various kinds
of things from buckshot to "salt bacon," and you have
drawn vivid pictures of being deprived of your pants
along with considerable flesh by a bulldog. But you were
brave and ran all the risks. You got ripe melons after
breaking open a green one or two, and they tasted better
than any you had ever eaten before or since.*

*The boys made a mistake by not taking advantage of
Judge Stockton's kind heart. If one had stood up in court
and said "Your Honor, did you ever swipe a watermelon
when you were a boy?" the Judge would undoubtedly
have been put in a bad position, for what boy ever grew
to manhood without the divine but dangerous pleasure of
transporting a watermelon from the patch to a cornfield?*

The boys truthfully said that everybody stole watermelons and there was no special harm in it.

Another reporting experience concerned the little nine-year-old girl who had acquired the dangerous habit of sniffing gasoline fumes until she "became dizzy and saw visions." Ed wrote:

She was found sitting by the roadside near her home pouring gasoline from a can and eagerly inhaling the fumes. The child confessed to her mother that she had been addicted to the practice for more than a year.

Today she was found beside a gasoline engine inhaling the fumes. She was in a stupor and talked of hearing queer voices. There was every evidence of gasoline intoxication. The little girl was sent by the court to a Juvenile home.

Another little girl, also nine years old, was sentenced to the reform school for girls at Chillicothe. Her father said she was "incorrigible." The deputy sheriff took the little girl in custody and boarded the night Wabash for Chillicothe. Ed limited his story to the bare facts and as a lawyer, could see that the law provided no alternatives in these sad cases.

On a happier note there was the story of "Little Blue Eyes," who wanted to see the big world:

Attired in a neat, white dress, her brown tresses freshly curled and her blue eyes hungering for a peep at the big world, little Miss Lois Peeler, daughter of Mr. and Mrs. J.E. Peeler, left the parental home this morning to gratify her wish to see more than the green grass in her father's lawn and to hear more than the song of the hens in the barnyard.

The little girl wandered down Cherry Street until her limbs became tired and finding a gate open, with the unconcern of childhood, she walked into the yard and sat upon the front porch. Presently she was noticed by Mrs. Samuel Dysart, into whose yard she had wandered, and while Mrs. Dysart was making every effort to ascertain the

88

identity of the child, its parents were ignorant of its whereabouts. The mother went about her household duties, thinking the little girl was with her father with whom she started to walk a short distance, as was her custom, when he left for town this morning. The father went about his work thinking the little girl had returned home, and neither knew differently until the father returned home at noon.

A search was immediately instituted in the neighborhood and, as it proved futile, the police were telephoned for and, with the assistance of central at the telephone office, the little girl was found and returned to her almost distracted parents.

Package of Gum

A sentimental man, Ed wrote about the "The Tribune's Most Cherished Christmas Gift":

The most cherished Christmas gift which the editor of the Daily Tribune has received, or will ever receive is a package of chewing gum. About a year ago the Tribune and a sweet-faced little fellow "took up" with each other. Cheery greetings and "howdy doos" cemented the friendship. Then the Tribune, occasionally, gave the little boy passes to the picture shows. The Tribune gives "passes" to a lot of little boys, but this particular sweet-faced and sweet-mannered little lad remembered. Today he came in and said: "Mr. Editor, what do you want for Christmas?" The editor assured his little friend that there was nothing specially he wanted. Then a look of disappointment came over the face of the boy and he added, "Ain't there nothin' you want?"

Then the editor, appreciating the fine feelings of the little fellow, in sheer desperation as to what he wanted that was commensurate with the lad's exchequer, told him that above every thing else he liked chewing gum. Out the boy went, but his gracious, discriminating spirit brought him back immediately. "What kind of gum do you like best? I want you to have what you want." We

89

answered, "Spearmint," and with a "Merry Christmas," a clasp of his little hand and a look in his eyes that played on your heart strings, he was gone.

There is no guile in a child. Children are strangers to dissembling and equivocation; their words and actions come straight from the heart, and deception is unknown to them.

Hence the little boy's gift to the Tribune is invaluable; more so than the wealth of Golconda, because it is unsought and unsullied, and from a little heart that knows nothing but purity and gratefulness.

This package of gum will never be "chewed." The editor will place it in memory's niche, and keep it till it's the oldest bunch of gum extant.

Watson was concerned about the high cost of marbles when he wrote an editorial on the subject titled: "Is There a Marble Trust?":

Agates that used to cost a dime now cost a quarter. "Comies" that used to run 100 for a nickel now run 50 for the same price. These startling facts were unearthed when the Daily Tribune conferred with a friend who had recently made purchases. Ask the first small boy you see what marbles cost. You will find the conditions as described.

Watson also was observant of conditions in the ice-skating sport. He had noticed that "some small boys are already looking over last year's skates to see if they are too short."

As much as Ed Watson liked children, he was always wary of the small boy and his snow balls:

No, you can't avoid the pernicious small boy with the ubiquitous snow-ball. If you run after him you get it in the eye, and he outsprints you; if you run away from him you get it in the neck.

Animals, as well as children, always attracted Ed's attention. There was the story about the Shetland pony which became stuck fast in some asphalt filler. Ed wrote:

Susie Smoke's pony was driven nearly up to the rope that is stretched across Broadway, and its feet adhered fast to the asphalt filler, which at this point had become only partially hardened. The little animal tried hard to free herself, but failed. Finally with some assistance, she got loose and lost no time getting away from what she evidently considered a dangerous locality. The pony was thoroughly frightened by the unusual experience, and trembled like a leaf for several minutes afterward. When on Broadway she still steps very gingerly on the paving.

In 1911 a Want Ad was placed in the *Tribune* inquiring about a place to board a child for the winter. Answers to the ad began to come in, numbering twenty. When told how many answers there were, two or three said: "Oh well, we can't get the child, then." Several said: "What we could get out of the board of the child doesn't amount to anything, but we want a child around the house." The person who inserted the Want Ad sent it in by mail.

"There are twenty answers hanging on the Want Ad hook for her," Watson said. "The circumstances show that little folks are an important factor around the house, and incidentally that advertisements in the Daily Tribune with its 2,500 subscribers bring results."

Throughout his life, Ed Watson was a patron of little boys. He handed out movie passes and football tickets to young Columbians with "casual abandon." After he bought one little boy an Indian suit, the store was besieged by the boy's playmates who ordered Indian suits to be charged to Watson's account.

Politics

A Staunch Democrat

"Ed Watson was a staunch Democrat." This was the statement of Jack Hackethorn, who left the *Tribune* for a stint as a photographer with Acme Pictures in Washington, D.C., and then with the *Detroit News.* Later he moved to St. Louis to work on the *Post-Dispatch,* and finally returned to Columbia to enter a related field, as a public relations man with the Missouri Farmers Association.

"Also," said Jack, "Col. Watson had integrity and he lived in a day of personal journalism. His editorials carried political weight over the state, and they were the Bible for his readers."

In the first issue of the *Tribune,* September 12, 1901, editor and founder of the *Tribune,* Charles Munro Strong, said:

> *In politics we do not expect to be rankly partisan or to enter the arena in aggressive form challenging controversy on political questions, but our stand will be with the Democratic Party whose principles we were brought up on, and to which we will endeavor to adhere.*

When Ed Watson took over the newspaper in 1905, his first issue dealt only with an announcement of general policy. Nothing was said about the *Tribune's* politics. Of course everyone knew that Watson was a Democrat, and that he had served as city attorney, winning the position on the Democratic ticket some years before.

Twelve days after Ed's announcement that he was taking over the *Tribune* as "Editor and Proprietor" he titled an editorial as "Talks With Our Readers." He still failed to mention politics.

During his first few months of publishing a newspaper he came out for Howard A. Gass, for State Superintendent of Schools on the Democratic ticket; he discussed the rise of Missouri in the politics of the nation; he noted the possibility that F.W. Niedermeyer, a Republican, might replace Samuel H. Elkins, also a Republican appointee of a Republican president who had received the nod for Columbia postmaster. He also chastised the Republicans for their support of high tariffs, and he floated a balloon for E.W. Stephens' Democratic candidacy for governor of the state in the coming election of 1908.

His interest in national politics was expressed in an editorial demanding direct vote of the people in the election of United States Senators:

> *The sooner the editors of the country begin to demand the election of the U.S. Senators by a direct vote of the people, the sooner the greatest foe to government by the people and for the people will be removed. If Senators were chosen by primaries instead of caucuses, would Aldrich, Foraker, Kean, Alger and other railroad and trust Senators, who admit with shameful frankness that they are representing Standard Oil, the railroads and the "interests," would they now be in the Senate, the foe to all legislation that stands for the "square deal?" The Senators, who control legislation are indifferent to adverse public opinion. To reform the Senate they must be defeated for re-election, and the way to do it is at the polls by a direct vote. Let Missouri take the lead in this matter.*

Ed Watson was a straight Democratic party ticket voter. He believed in his party and opposed, nationally or locally, anyone who tried to dissuade him from the straight line of Democratic voting. He wrote:

Does anyone think for a minute that were the Republicans in the ascendancy in Columbia that the Democrats would receive recognition for a minute or even have a look in for political preferment? Not a bit of it. Republicans are not built that way. The argument for partisan politics in municipal government is peculiarly strong for Republicans in Columbia. Democrats would probably advocate non-partisanism just as vehemently were they in the minority.

It was common for Watson to travel in the interest of the Democratic party. On occasion he was a delegate to conventions, but mostly he attended meetings of the party for the purpose of drumming up interest in it. He felt particularly at home at the meetings in St. Louis, where he had learned about city life as a reporter. When the State Democratic Committee moved the state headquarters back to the old Laclede Hotel, he became lyrical in his praise of the move:

At the Planters Hotel, even the genial host, Col. Landrum, doing everything in his power for the comfort and accommodation of visiting Democrats, there was an air of constraint among the old timers. Most of them tiptoed around and talked in undertones. Everything was a wee bit too fine and in painful contrast to the free and easy atmosphere of the Laclede.

"If one wanted to spit," Watson wrote, "several steps would probably be necessary to land in the big two-story brass cuspidors that are always kept bright and shiny at the Planters. At the Laclede they are flat and broad and roomy and easy to hit. And then," he added, "it didn't make much difference if a bad shot missed one of them a foot or two."

He continued:

At the Planters, there were prayer meeting manners except when adjournment was taken to the bar and then some of the boys were apt to take water in their whiskey. Many attribute the defeat of the Democratic Party to the fact that free communication between the faithful could not be had under these circumstances and refreshments diluted to such an extent that the proper degree of devine afflatus could not be secured to produce the enthusiasm that has always landed the Democracy a winner in Missouri.

At the Laclede this will be different. The old-timers have hailed the change with joy. They will flock to the old hostelry, spit where they list, cock their feet where they please, and plan for Democratic victory next fall. Again, we are glad that the Democracy has gotten back to the old headquarters, and victory is certain in the fall.

In the old "old days" when politicians were brought around to meet *Tribune* employees, the bigger and more important the candidates were, the more likely that they would be brought around to be introduced. Every candidate for Democratic Governor of the state, and a few Republicans, from 1905 to 1937, were escorted through this ceremony of hand-shaking and, being good politicians, they enjoyed it. The employees, too, enjoyed these little acts of courtesy.

Assessors Are Human

Throughout Watson's life he campaigned for reforms in the political field. One reform he hoped for was the change in law to make the term of the county assessor four years instead of two. In 1913 he wrote:

One of the bills introduced into the legislature that should become a law is that which makes the term of a County Assessor four years and then makes him ineligible for re-election. There are many things to commend this measure becoming a law. All assessors are human and it is a constant temptation to electioneer a bit for re-election. On this account they are very apt to favor the tax-paying voter in levying assessments against his property, especially if the property owner is an influential one that takes interest in politics. It is the most natural thing in the world and most any man would be acting in a manner subconsciously when he did it. On this account the above gives assessors a term that amounts to as much as two terms under the present law and removes any temptation for favoritism that may exist. The Daily Tribune has advocated the law from time to time in its editorial columns.

Student Voting

Occasionally illegal voting of students was challenged. It caused some bitterness between "town and gown." Ed, who always backed the University in its many endeavors, including financial, nevertheless was considered a part of the "town." To this end he wrote:

A certain member of the University faculty who was born and reared in Columbia is reported to have said prior to the election of Monday, "Smash the town, it has never done anything for the University. We don't care anything about harmony with the townspeople." If this remark was made by the gentleman who is alleged to have made it, it could not have been made otherwise than maliciously for he has been a resident of Columbia all his life and knows the history of the University as well as anyone in Boone County. Hence he knows that Boone County practically supported the State University until 1867, and that it continued even after that date to help support it and that the first substantial recognition the University ever received from the state was after the fire of 1892, and if he will stop to think a minute he will remember that one of his kinsmen headed the list with $1,000 when Columbia bought the University for the second time by subscribing $50,000 in 1892, after having paid $139,000 for it in 1839. And yet Columbia has never done anything for the University!

Last Saloon Closes

Watson was opposed to Local Option or Prohibition, whichever term was in current use. "In the last analysis," he said, "local option is prohibition and it is doing violence to the intelligence of anyone to seek to convince otherwise." On January 2, 1908, two of Columbia's saloons closed and the other one would be out of business within another week. Ed wrote:

> The Tribune has never been equivocal or uncertain in its utterance on any proposition. On the subject of local option, this paper has decided opinions. It believes that the best way to handle the liquor question is through the medium of high license...the Tribune is prepared to pass by the usual statements and insinuations that the opponents of local option and prohibition are advocates of intemperance and saloons. It is to be hoped that a sober and sane discussion will precede the elections on Februrary 5. The Tribune will do what it can to prevent personalities and ill feeling, and settle the vexed question involved so that there can be no unpleasant aftermaths.

Two Columbia leaders, one of whom was Ed Watson's close friend, University President R.H. Jesse, and the other Ed's brother-in-law Dean H.J. Waters, were speakers at a local option meeting at the Boone County courthouse in January prior to the February election. Ed objected to their statements, calling them "flimsy arguments."

The local option people pulled out all the stops and brought in Mrs. Nellie Berger, of neighboring Clark, Mo., who was national president of the Womens Christian Temperance Union. Mrs. Berger gave a talk at the University auditorium, which was filled with students. Later when there was much student voting, the votes were challenged and Watson published several editorials on the "menace of student voting." Ed wrote:

> The matter of allowing students to vote in Columbia is serious. If they are given this privilege, control of the city's affairs by the citizens of Columbia will become impossible...the laws of Missouri expressly state that no student of an educational institution gains or loses a residence by reason of that fact. This is given in Section 7, Article 8. The statute is clear and unequivocal...the Tribune believes deeply in the old Democratic principle that the law has nothing to do with the personal liberties of the indi-

vidual and when it seeks to invade his private rights by sumptuary legislation, at that moment is violence done the deep-seated and broad principles of government which Jefferson and his compatriots gave to the world in the Magna Carta of the new world. The founders of this Government never intended or thought of it being prostituted to the extent of "one man's conscience being the guide to another's conduct." They and the men upon whom their mantles fell, always rebuked and deprecated any such tendencies, and there were attempts in their times just as there are today.

Cheer Up Bachelors!

As serious as Watson was concerning prohibition and the law, he managed to see bits of humor in the proposed so-called Bachelor Tax and he directed an editorial to his fellow bachelors:

Cheer up Bachelors! There is still balm in Gilead should local option by a miracle win the day. Some one has suggested that the $50 bachelor tax is cheaper than keeping house, anyway.

Two days later Columbia went dry by 42 votes. The count was 998 to 956. And Ed wrote:

The Tribune is satisfied with the fight it made against local option. It has no regrets except as to the result. It would pursue the same course were a similar contest to come up next week. It expects to oppose prohibition as a matter of principle whenever and wherever the question comes up for determination. There will be no grumbling, however, by the Tribune over milk that is spilled. One Mr. Iago once very wisely observed: "To mourn a mischief that is past and gone is the best way to draw new mischief on. What can not be preserved when fortune takes, patience her injury, a mockery makes. The robbed that smiles steals something from the thief. He robs himself who spends a bootless grief."

The loss of the saloons cut off $6,000 from the city's revenue. Ed wrote that the money had to be made up in some manner because "the city cannot run on credit indefinitely":

The city of Columbia needs more money. The need is not to be put aside like a family skeleton and thought of once in a while. It is an imperative need that must be met. Columbia needs more water mains and more light extensions, better machinery at the city water and light plant, more fire protection, enough money to pay city bills on the dot and lay over a part of the city's expense bill to await more money.

The loss of $6,000 saloon revenue, no matter what anyone says on the subject, has created an additional burden on the city revenues. The city has borrowed money, and borrowed money, to meet current expenses. This policy can not be continued indefinitely.

General Fabius' Policy

When the next local option election came around the *Tribune* was not so actively involved and gave this explanation:

The Tribune has been asked why it isn't so militant in this local option campaign as it was in the last. It isn't that the Tribune has changed one jot or one tittle in the views regarding prohibition. A certain Roman general, Fabius Maximus, was the undoing of Hannibal, the Carthagenian, just because he wouldn't fight the great general when he wanted him to. Hannibal followed the retreating Fabius far into the interior of Italy. The Carthagenian finally ran out of supplies and provisions and his ultimate defeat was the result of the tactics of Fabius. The latter's methods have henceforth been known as the "Fabian Policy." In other words, fighting is sometimes less effective than it is generally thought to be. It is sometimes necessary, but at all times disagreeable.

The "drys" carried the day again and Ed became philosophical:

100

There are a good many reasons advanced as to why the county went "dry." One of the late Gov. Bob Taylor's favorite stories was about a man who was thrown down stairs by two or three other gentlemen whom he had displeased. After wondering a long time what was the reason for their belligerency, he finally decided that it was because they didn't want him up there.

Reasoning by analogy, it's altogether probable that the county went "dry" because the people wanted it that way.

John Barleycorn Dies

In January 1919, "while the soldiers were fighting in France," the nation passed the Eighteenth Amendment and the country was dry, officially. It took another year for the law to become reality but the nation's citizenry immediately began getting its liquor from speakeasies, back alleys and homebrew basements.

On January 16, 1920, the *Tribune* ran the following headline:

A DRY AMERICA AT 12:01 A.M. TOMORROW
The sub-head read:

DREAMS OF REFORMERS BECOME
A REALITY AS JOHN BARLEYCORN DIES

* * *

The Al Smith Editorial

Rowland Smith, long-time *Tribune* reporter, who had succeeded Clyde Duncan as reporter on the University beat, remembered the "Al Smith editorial" as the one attracting the most national attention. William Allen White had his "What's Wrong with Kansas" editorial; Ed Watson was equally famous throughout the country for his editorial, "The Great Tragedy."

On the morning following Al Smith's loss in his race for the presidency, Watson bought an Orthophonic Victrola and one record. He sat the record player on a table outside the front office door on South Ninth Street, where foot traffic was the heaviest in town. He then took his chair outside, propped it against the wall, cranked the Victrola, inserted his one record in the machine, and played Smith's favorite song, "The Sidewalks of New York." He sat there most of the morning, with his black, derby hat askew, playing the record over and over, regardless of the stares of curious students and others passing by.

That afternoon his editorial came out in the *Tribune* and was widely reprinted over the nation. Copies of the editorial were mailed by Al Smith fans throughout the country. It follows:

THE GREAT TRAGEDY

"Ill fares the land, to sickening ills a prey," where bigotry, prohibition and intolerance holds sway.

The people of the United States by an overwhelming majority yesterday—a landslide—endorsed corruption in office, thievery, bribery, demagoguery, charlatanism, dishonesty, looting the government of its natural resources, and all of the general cussedness of which Republican party leaders have been guilty during the past seven and a half years. The stamp of approval has been placed on that traitor to his country's interest, former Secretary of Interior Fall; bribe givers Sinclair and Doheny; Forbes, who stole the money appropriated for the comfort and welfare of the wracked, maimed and suffering soldiers of the World War who saved their country and Europe from the despot's heel; recreant, dishonest, purloining Attorney General Daugherty, and his henchman and man Friday, Jess Smith, not to mention the Ohio Gang which President Harding took as a retinue and preyed like vultures on the public moneys, and like "cut-purses of the empire put it in their pockets." This is what the people of the country want, including renegade and derelict Demo-

crats, as indicated by their votes, what they endorse and desire. The vox populi has said this is right, proper and preferable. They have again given sanction to robbing and plundering, buried an honest, constructive progressive citizen and given idiotic and gourd-head approval of a man who was a resident and business man of another country until ten years ago, who did not cast a vote in the land that gave him birth until he was 45 years old, and who should have been repatriated and made to wait the usual period required of foreigners before he was allowed to exercise the right of suffrage here, expatriated as he had been for over twenty years. May they reap a belly-full of what they voted for.

As to the Republican corn belt farmer: For eight years he has been a beggar and a mendicant, bellowing and moaning for relief from his untoward economic condition; praying for help from two Republican administrations; he asked for bread and has been given stone—fed on promises and persiflage. All tore their pants for the McNary-Haugen bill, swore and be damned they'd get even with the Republican party in November. What happened? A high tariff on their products was promised as one of many Republican panaceas for the rehabilitation of the agricultural interests and they were fed up by Viscount Hoover with the statement that he would call an extra session of Congress for their especial and immediate relief, and simple dolts and gimlet-heads, as they have always been, they believed this recent importation from Merry England. The fool way-faring man should, and does, know that the farmer of this country exports the five principal products that are his bread and meat, his very subsistence and life and blood. This surplus helps immeasurably to make the mare go. It is common knowledge, primer economics, that the inexorable law of supply and demand makes impossible any benefit whatsoever from a tariff on commodities of which there is a surplus and which must be exported if anything is to be realized from them. Yet the Farm Belt clod buster swallowed it all like fish and forgot all about his dicer's oath regarding the McNary-Haugen bill, his sworn intention about evening up the Republican party on November 6th, and again fawningly licked the hand of the party that has made him all but a serf and a peon. The best thing these misguided and witless farmers who voted for Hoover can do is to dig in, leave off going to town every day or so, and remove some of the lead from the seat of their trousers. This will get them immeasurably more than waiting for the Republican party to give them aid by co-operative marketing, the McNary-Haugen bill, or through any other of the specious promises and vain plans which are as numerous with Hoover and his party as "leaves in Valambrosa." Furthermore, they deserve no better fate than that about which they have been bellyaching for eight years past.

The Democrats in their hour of defeat have the satisfaction and gratification that theirs was a gallant and a militant fight for the people of our great country; that they were led by a gallant, fearless American who fought his own fight for what he stood for, compares as Hyperion to a Satyr to the Republican candidate who, Quaker-like, feared the challenge of his adversary and would not defend what principles and program he stood for except by proxy. The Democrats can rejoice that theirs was a clean fight made by superior men and women; that they had no support from the discredited and rotten Anti-Saloon League, the bootleggers, the meddling Methodists who should remove the beam from their own eye as to linking church and state before they point an accusing finger at the Roman Catholics. It would probably be better for the country to bow to the Pope than a Methodist Bishop. To this list might be added the bigots and the intolerants.

But —

"The robbed that smiles steals something from the thief; he robs himself who spends a bootless grief."

So Democrats will bide their time and watch confidently for Herbert Hoover to wreck the Republican party and reap the damning of the people who elected him. Lincoln's aphorism regarding the astuteness and common sense of the people comes to mind.

Sports

Throughout Watson's life he demonstrated his great interest in sports, both as an active participant and as a spectator. Football and baseball were his favorites. As with sports fans everywhere, he liked to win, and near the end of his first year of ownership of the *Tribune,* and at the end of the football season, he was ready for the Tigers to give up the game. In November 1906, he wrote an editorial entitled; "LET'S QUIT":

> *The game of football Saturday in which Missouri went down to inglorious defeat before Washington was enough to make a strong man weep. Now is the first rate time for Missouri to quit playing football. It is probably imperative to play Kansas as a contract to do so exists.*

Four days later Ed was still fuming. He was particularly unhappy with the director of athletics, Dr. Clark W. Hetherington, whom he called a "Dictator." Watson wrote:

> *That the article of football which the University has been putting up, almost 'till the mind of man runneth not to the contrary is a disgrace to the institution, all will admit. When the management of athletics at Kansas University states that Missouri University is too puny a rival for the Jayhawkers to waste time with, when the eleven which the University puts in the field each year is the standing joke of the football world, despite the "moral victories," it is time to quit and turn our attention to ping-pong, tiddledy winks and croquet. Under the present conditions and the present management the loyal sons of the University will be forced to continued eating the husks of*

football glory and, like Ichabod, "walk backward, with averted head, to hide the shame."

Watson also opposed the idea of giving the big M for sports only. He wrote:

> *It always seemed strange to me that the Athletic Department has usurped to itself the sole right to bestow the University letter on a student. Are athletes the only fitting representatives of "Fair Missouri?" If we can judge by the grades and manners of some of them they are certainly not. Indeed, that theory is all nonsense. The "M" should be the symbol of those things that the present diploma is too narrow to take into account. Give it to big football men—if they are big men; to debaters who win debates; and in general to those men who "do things" for the school. Don't let the "M" stand for the measure of a man's muscle. Let it mean big, broad-minded, brainy, all-around "Missouri Men."*

The Athletic Department also was chastised by Ed for the management's intention to erect a wooden fence, fifteen feet in height, along Rollins Street on the north side of Rollins Field. Athletic directors have always, through the years, explored various avenues for raising money. This time the curators and athletic director wanted to sell ads on the fence and also keep non-paying customers from witnessing games outside the Field. Ed wrote:

> *It is contended by property owners that the intent of the board and the athletic management is to make money by flaring advertisements of patent medicines and of local businesses. The fence would be unsightly and be anything but a pleasing prospect for the residents in that pretty part of town to gaze at continuously. It is also true that the high fence would shut out the south breeze in summer and make that part of town less comfortable to live in.*

In the end the idea of erecting a wooden fence with advertising was dropped.

Columbia's first look at night baseball, called "Evening Baseball," came on September 7, 1906. The game was played at Rollins Field with a Columbia team, the "Reds," playing a team composed of Cherokee Indians, who carried with them "a complete lighting plant." The Cherokee team was one of the strongest semi-professional teams in the Southwest, and had defeated all comers.

MU-KU Football Rivalry

The Missouri-Kansas football rivalry which began in 1891 was from the beginning a knock-down-drag-out fight, but Missouri had won only three of eighteen games up to and including the 1908 game. Chancellor Strong of the University of Kansas commented that "no malice now exists against Missouri from the pillaging of Lawrence during the Civil War because we are getting revenge from Missouri every Thanksgiving Day game." Ed wrote:

The Kansas game is the criterion for Missouri rooters. Since the days when "Pop" Bliss coached the Missouri team that licked Northwestern, Vanderbilt, Purdue, Iowa, Kansas and pretty much everything in the neighborhood of Missouri that looked like a football team, excuses have been multiplying at the University.

William Roper, former Princetonian, was hired as the Missouri coach for the 1909 season at the then considerable salary of $2,500. Watson immediately backed the new coach in an editorial that ended with: "May Roper see his charges lick Kansas on Thanksgiving Day."

Coach Roper arrived September 20 and by the end of November he and "his charges" had won the Missouri Valley title, and that included, best of all, the defeat of K.U. 12-6. Ed wrote: "Mister Roper's trouncing of Kansas yesterday has solved the Democratic gubernatorial nominee problem." By this time Watson had forgotten all about his desire to scrap football at Missouri. In fact he was ready to enter the big time:

There is no reason for the University of Missouri to play a string of second rate colleges at football. Since that sport rouses more widespread interest and advertises the University more than any other form of inter-collegiate athletics, the advertising should be in quarters where it will do the most good. Dr. R.H. Jesse, before retiring from the presidency of the institution on account of broken health, asserted that Missouri University should rate high in the South and the Southwest, because it is essentially the leading Southern university, as well as a leading Western university. New students are to be drawn from the South and Southwest. Missouri should therefore add to her football schedule such teams as Vanderbilt, Oklahoma, Texas and Arkansas.

Roper was a one-year man at Missouri because Princeton offered him twice Missouri's salary, and Watson said that "Missouri fans were Roper-mad and wanted him back at any price." Nevertheless, Roper was succeeded by Bill Hollenback, who had coached Pennsylvania State, and Watson wrote: "It would be hard to find a man better equipped for the job of teaching the gold and black warriors how to drub the Jayhawks."

Missouri defeated Oklahoma 26-0 and Washington U. 27-3, but on Turkey Day in Kansas City, against Kansas U., Missouri could gain only a tie, 5-5. *Tribune* headlines read: "OFFICIALS BEAT TIGERS—M.U. WON." But the score remained a tie in the record books. Ed wrote:

It is the general belief of all who saw the game that the officials either had money bet against Missouri or were prejudiced in favor of Kansas for some other reason, as no more one-sided decisions were ever seen in a football game in which Missouri took part. Kansas is a pretty hard football nut to crack even when the game is played "on the level." But when the umpire of the game is the bright particular star for the Jayhawkers the task of beating them nearly resolves itself into an impossibility.

The 1910 game was the last one between K.U. and M.U. to

be held in Kansas City. The Missouri Valley Conference, meeting at DesMoines, Iowa, ruled that the Turkey Day game should be played in Columbia and Lawrence, with Columbia getting the 1911 game. Missouri began to get ready for the contest, and installed a new concrete stadium to seat 4,125 persons. Forty men did the stadium-building work.

Beat Kansas Signs Impolite?

The Columbia Commercial Club decided that the "Beat Kansas" signs that were going up all over downtown Columbia were "impolite" and would have to come down. Watson did not agree with the club's decision and said so:

> The Daily Tribune believes that the utmost courtesy should be shown our guests from Kansas when they visit Columbia Friday and Saturday. It deprecates any inclination whatsoever to treat them in any but a generous and sportsmanlike manner and it hopes there will be no instances where rules of gentlemanly conduct are transgressed. But the Tribune also thinks that the action of the Commercial Club in passing resolutions asking that all "Beat Kansas" legends be torn down and all buttons of the same kind discarded is straining the matter somewhat and is a kind of saturated solution of courtesy that is unnecessary. It is a kind of Gaston and Alphonse brand of politeness that is a trifle hyperbolous and smacks a little of insincerity. A "Beat Kansas" shibboleth will not offend our friends from the Sunflower State, as experience has taught that they are not so thin-skinned and sensitive as all that. Courteous treatment should, and will be accorded them, but the down with the "Beat Kansas" signs is drawing it a little fine.

The signs stayed up. The game was played but the attendance was poor. "Bleeding Kansas came not," Ed wrote. The score, once more, was a tie 3-3.

Quantrell Days Recalled

The rivalry between Missouri and Kansas continued, and three years later, when Missouri Beat Kansas at Lawrence, Ed wrote:

The 10-7 result Saturday startled the inhabitants of Lawrence, Kansas, more than anything that has happened since the visit of Quantrell in 1862.

From time to time, Watson berated the *Kansas City Star* for its "disloyalty" to Missouri and its "favoritism" shown Kansas. After the M.U. win over Kansas in 1916, Ed wrote:

Was it not a pity, when Col. William Nelson—peace to his memory—who formulated the plans which are now the policy of the Star, did not take his few fonts of type and his rattling old press across the Missouri River and locate in Kansas City, Kan., after he left his old home in Indiana so precipitately, instead of anchoring on the Missouri side of the river.

In spite of Watson's loyalty to Missouri, he was ever ready to display his usual courtesy, brought to Missouri by his ancestors from the Commonwealth of Virginia. An editorial in 1922 illustrates his thoroughly ingrained Southern hospitality:

It is told of two Irishmen, with a natural and lasting antipathy each toward the other, a state of belligerency which had embroiled them long and often, that one of them lay sick seemingly unto death. The parish priest was about to extend extreme unction to the ailing one, but before he did so, he very much desired that his two belligerant parishoners should become reconciled to each other and that amity and good feeling should exist between them before the failing one took the long trail. He accordingly summoned the one in good health to the bedside of the supposedly dying one, where, in a tearful reconciliation, each forgave the other for all past differences and expressed sorrow and regret and forgiveness. Mike was leaving what was thought to be the deathbed of Pat, shaking with emotion. Pat called to him: "But Mike, remember that this don't go if I rises from me sick bed."

But we of Missouri extend a cordial greeting and a sincere welcome to our guests from Kansas. It might be observed in passing that this was written before the game. We might possibly have a modicum of the sentiments of Pat if beaten, but welcome, and our extension of the glad hand goes, just the same.

Mo-Kan Boys In Same War

Following the game, which Missouri won 9-7, Watson began to analyze the Missouri-Kansas confrontation with a mellowing of attitude. He wrote:

One fortunate situation has developed in the annual Missouri-Kansas football game, and that is the elimination of that hatred between the two teams left over from the Civil War. There has been another great war, and in this Missouri and Kansas boys fought together in one of the best divisions that went overseas. The memories of the hardships they endured together, the great fight for the common cause and a better acquaintance emanating from closer social intercourse brought understanding and real sportsmanship between the two schools. The Kansas team and the Kansas rooters are true sportsmen and play the game in the manner of such.

111

Boosting a Town

A Park Is Needed

Watson had owned the *Tribune* not quite nine months when he began his drive for a park for Columbia. Neither he nor most of the other citizens of the town recalled that a small park, named Jeannette Park, had been given to the city in 1904 by General Odon Guitar. Ed's editorial, titled "A Shortcoming of Columbia," stated:

> There is not a public park in the city or outside it. The University campus in a measure has answered the purposes, but it is only quasi-public. Columbia should have a place of public recreation and amusement of this kind. Many cities less pretentious have resorts of this nature with deep wells, small lakes and all necessary appointments. Until Columbia enterprise secures one for Columbia we will always be handicapped in holding Chautauquas or any other public function of this nature.

A new park plan was presented to the city council in 1911, but Ed opposed the plan. He wrote:

> Columbia has long been in need of a public park and the time is not far distant when this need will become recognized as a necessity, but a thoughtful consideration of the present financial condition of the city, renders such a contemplation as the purchase of land for park purposes utterly ridiculous.

Eight Years later, in 1919, Ed again decided to editorialize upon the need for a park. He still did not know about the existence of Jeannette Park, and he wrote:

113

The city administration has no money with which to buy a small park, and appearances are that if within the next few years Columbia gets a park it will have to come in some other manner. There are men and women in Columbia who could donate the land and the council could probably find enough money from year to year to beautify it.

Jeannette Park Discovered

In August of that year, City Clerk John Bicknell dusted off his records and proved that Jeannette Park, at Grand and Second avenues, really did exist. General Guitar had given the 146x135 foot park to the city on August 6, 1904 when he subdivided his old homestead, "Eagle's Nest," in North Columbia. Ed wrote:

Perhaps Columbia's little park would still be in the wilderness of weeds except for the weed-cutting ordinance.

Cut the Weeds

The weed-cutting ordinance was another pet project of Ed's and resulted in his demand that the law be enforced. On the first day of the 1906 weed-cutting season, he warned that there "is an ordinance requiring the weeds be cut, and those who do not comply with it will be prosecuted in the police court." Later he wrote: "Weeds make a town look like a small boy with his hair uncombed." He also maintained that "weeds are harborers of disease and threaten the health of a community. There are too many in Columbia."

Three years later, Ed was still talking about weed-cutting but some discouragement was indicated when he wrote:

The "cut the weeds" season has begun. Newspapers will endeavor to stir up civic pride enough to induce citizens to remove the unsightly and unhealthy growth along the sidewalks and streets, but the weeds will increase in size

114

and flourish like the proverbial green bay tree until Jack Frost himself trims them.

In 1919, after year in and year out pleading with people and cajoling them to cut their weeds, he wrote a front page headline:

PROMINENT CITIZENS ARRESTED TODAY:

The story concerned fourteen citizens who had failed to cut their weeds and Ed printed all fourteen names.

* * *

First Car Owners In Columbia

In 1905 the year that Ed Watson bought the *Tribune* five automobiles were purchased by residents of Columbia. Four years later, only thirty automobiles plied the mostly mud streets of the town. The first car was owned by W.B. West, a machine shop proprietor, who bought the license for his new car June 5, 1905. The car was a lever-drive runabout. The other cars, bought the same year, were owned by Hugh Stephens, J.E. Morse, John E. Bishop and F.A. Sampson. "All of the cars were regarded with curious eyes by Columbians and many horses snorted and backed away from the chugging motor cars," according to Watson.

By 1909 Ed had written about the two-seated, 22-horsepower machine, "The Rambler," purchased by S.A. Schrock, "the first red devil to thread the streets of Columbia." Other cars, bought in a four-year period, were: Reo, Cadillac, Ford, Moon, Buick, Great Western, Mitchell, Rapid, Dorris, Maxwell, Kline, Haynes, Peerless and Pierce-Arrow. About this time the Columbia City Council ordered an eight dollar stop watch for the police to register the time on auto speeders.

In 1910 E.W. Stephens and his three sons, Hugh, J.L.,

and Sydney, made a tour of the county in Hugh's Dorris. The *Tribune* ran a story describing the trip:

> *The party started at eight o'clock and went by way of the Rocheport Gravel, Model Farm, Woodlandville, Harrisburg, Sturgeon, Centralia, Youngers, returning through the Glenn neighborhood, reaching home at 5:30 in the afternoon. The distance was eighty-two miles. A feature of the trip which gave it a bit of sentiment was that they lunched on the banks of Cedar Creek, bordering the farm of their grandfather and great grandfather, the late Elijah Stephens. They also visited the old Stephens homestead and the family cemetery nearby.*

"Company" of Scouts

Also in the year 1910, when the Boy Scout movement was brought to this country from England, Columbia citizens held a discussion of the movement on November 29 at the Christian Church. It was decided to organize a "company" of scouts. This was the beginning of good times and bad times for the scouts during the next nine years. During that period "companies" were organized and re-organized. A favorite hike was down the Katy tracks to Brushwood Lake. Another trip of longer duration was spearheaded by Tiger football coach H.F. Schulte to Niangua River near Hahatonka. This was a two-week trip and the scouts and their leaders went by train from Columbia to Bagnell, by way of Jefferson City. The trip from Bagnell to Linn Creek village was made by boat, then on to the camp by hiking. The Linn Creek camp was used each summer for the next five years, from 1919 to 1924, by the Columbia scouts. It was a beautiful area, as it is today, the change being that the Lake of the Ozarks now covers the bottoms of the Osage River and its tributary streams, including the Big and Little Niangua rivers and Linn Creek.

116

Electric RR—Wave of Future

The advent of the automobile brought the promise of good roads, but before that, the Electric Railroad was considered "the wave of the future." In 1906 many electric railroad "balloons" were tested, and Watson editorially hoped that the so-called County Seat Electric Railroad between St. Louis and Kansas City proved not to be "a passing bubble." An electric line right-of-way was built from Mexico to Rowena in Audrain County and it was thought that this road would be extended through Hereford, Callaway County, to Columbia. Another planned electric road was to Jefferson City by way of Ashland. Two years later, with none of the roads any more than on paper, Ed wrote:

Many railroad rumors have been afloat of late, all of them involving Columbia. Many such rumors have proved idle dreams in the past, but "where there is much smoke there is some fire," and it seems likely that railroad builders are sufficiently interested in the Burlington project to produce results.

A year later there still was much talk and little action. Watson wrote:

When an electric railway comes to Columbia, it will in all probability run down Broadway, but we don't want freight cars down Broadway!

Watson thought, and said, that "railroad promoters have their place, and the fact that sometimes they skip out without the formality of leaving any forwarding address is not wholly bad." One such promoter "breezed into Columbia about two years ago, from where no one knew, and announced that the company he was organizing would build an electric line from Mexico to Columbia and thence to Ashland. It was currently reported, and generally believed, that he was a fake."

117

He blazed the way, did the preliminary work and like many original promoters slipped a cog and departed for green fields and pastures new. His place has been taken by a substantial financier who will not be bothered with blazing the way. The promoter has a function to perform and he performed it. The road will probably be built. So some good can come out of Nazareth after all.

Watson ended the above editorial on an optimistic note, but he was not be be hoodwinked by railroad promoters, large or small, as witness his remarks about the comments of a railroad director:

A director of the St. Louis and Kansas City Electric Railway Company recently made the statement that the electric railroad company would make an Indianapolis out of Columbia. Who cares?

Newspaper Railroads

By 1914, with more than a hundred automobiles in Columbia, and thousands throughout the state, the Electric Railroad boom was still booming, and Ed talked about "Newspaper Railroads:"

Railroads (in the newspapers) are covering Central Missouri with their lace-like tracery, the surveyors have arrived, the work is about to begin and will be pushed in "actual construction," as the stories say, to make assurance doubly sure.

Those who remember the champion railroad liars who have visited our prosperous little city will recall how it was possible, while the promoters talked, to squint the eyes somewhat, and see the glittering on the rails.

Regarding these railroads, the much-fagged credulity of Columbia is in the state of mind well exemplified by the old time anecdote that differentiates the meaning between "hope" and "expect" wherein Johnnie's mother, in response to his entreaty for a sentence illustrating the

118

meaning of the two words for use in his grammar lesson next day, replied: "Johnnie, I hope to see your Pa in Heaven, but I don't expect to."

But there—maybe the railroads are coming this year.

Early Hotels and Taverns

In Boone's Lick Trail days, Columbia taverns, or hotels, were located on or near Broadway. Stage coach arrivals were events eagerly awaited, and it could be expected that there would be an assemblage of citizens on hand to welcome the passengers.

When the Wabash railroad came into Columbia, the important hostelry of the city was the Powers House, at Tenth and Walnut streets, one block from the Wabash depot. The Central Hotel, Sixth and Broadway, and the West End Hotel on Broadway between Fifth and Sixth streets, took care of the Katy passengers. There were also hacks available for delivery of hotel customers to other places such as the Gordon Hotel, originally called the Cottage Hotel, Tenth and Cherry streets, the old Columbia Hotel on Eighth Street and the Winn House.

Six months after Ed Watson took over the *Tribune*, he was writing on the need for more hotel rooms in Columbia:

Never in the history of Columbia has there been such a need for hotel rooms as at present. There has scarcely been a night that passengers on the Wabash and the M.K.&T. have been able to secure a room, unless it was shared with some one else, always a stranger.

The hacks drive to the first hotel and the guest registers. All guests ask for a good room. At the first place the clerk will express his regret that he is unable to give the guest a room. He will, however, do the best he can, and that is to put him in a room with another gentleman. The guest takes his grip, calls the hack and goes to one of the other hostelries. Here he registers and repeats his request for a room. The clerk is sorry but the best he can do is furnish a cot in the parlor. The guest again grabs his grips and

119

again takes the hack for another hotel. Here he is told that the best possible accommodation that can be given him is a cot in the hall.

The above has actually been the experience of many who have visited Columbia lately. Traveling salesmen, many of them who do not telegraph for a room, endeavor to get in and out of Columbia in a day. Those who have had the experience above mentioned a time or two do not care to risk it again. They, of course, tell other traveling men Columbia's hotels are good, but the hotel capacity of the town is sadly lacking.

Athens Hotel

About six months later H.H. Tandy decided to add extra rooms to the old Athens Hotel at Ninth and Walnut streets, to make it a 100-room hotel. His building plans were given to the *Tribune:*

"The general architecture of the building will conform to that of the present Athens. I have been waiting on the lease of the Chandler & Court Livery Barn to expire next spring and I will begin work on the new building. It will be a large modern hotel, three stories with a basement and a frontage on Walnut of 160 feet. The depth will be 142 and one-half feet. The hotel will be as up-to-date as I can make it and will correspond with the improvements recently made in Columbia and with the progressive spirit of the town. Columbia has long needed a large up-to-date hotel and I shall do my best to give it one. There is no better place for one than here."

Several years later, with the Athens only a 75-room hotel, there was still a need for more hotel rooms, and there were many companies attempting to organize. Cited by these companies as good locations they were planning to build on included Ninth and Locust streets, headed by Capt. S.A. Smoke; another at Sixth and Broadway by Judge J.A. Stewart; another by T.S. Gordon, owner of the Gordon Hotel, on a site not made public;

and another on the site of the Powers House that burned in June 1913. The Athens Hotel announced the same day of the Powers House fire that it would build an additional 25 rooms to achieve the long-awaited 100-room hotel it had promised, and the contract was let to Emmett Fay the following month.

Ed was still unhappy with the progress in hotel building. He commented editorially:

> The hotels of the past have been built principally in the newspapers, the walls of which have been "hot air" and the roof "blue sky." If the promoters of the hotel project would get as busy as Dame Rumor has been today, by the first of December a magnificent hotel would grace some one of the excellent hotel sites in Columbia.

Daniel Boone Tavern

The year was 1913, and after two more years of proposals for hotels from interests, Columbia finally had a proposed hotel, dependant only on a popular subscription of $8,000. Ed wrote:

> The new hotel, to be called the Daniel Boone Hotel, will be of re-inforced concrete construction, fireproof in every way. It will be located at the corner of Seventh and Broadway and will cost $100,000. Only $8,000 will be needed to be raised by popular subscription. No stores will occupy the ground floor, which will be devoted to a large and luxuriously appointed lobby, and smoking rooms. There will be a mezzanine floor. Financing the hotel is Louis W. Dumas Jr. The location on Broadway has an advantage that can not be overlooked during the automobile tourist season. Automobilists who pass a five-story, modern Hotel in a town as good looking as Columbia, to stop elsewhere will be rare indeed. Columbians have been importunate for several years in their desire to obtain a hotel that will "match up" with Columbia; columns upon columns have been written about the crying shame that we had none. Now here is a chance that any other live town in America would jump at. If Columbia

people do not embrace it, they should henceforth hold their peace concerning a modern hostelry equal to "our needs."

For many years Watson had attempted to obtain a statue of Daniel Boone for the city and county. At last here was the memorial he was looking for, not a statue to be sure, but as he said, "a fitting marker to the memory of the man."

What better monument could be erected to Daniel Boone than the modern, five-story hotel planned for Columbia? Standing on the old Booneslick Road itself, fronting the pathway over which the long rifle pioneers pressed forward in their conquest of the wilderness, it will be a fitting marker to the memory of the man for whom the old county is named.

What though the deer trail is now paved with brick, and a town of 14,000 inhabitants stands on the spot where a few lone cabins and a frontier blockhouse marked the first settlement? That the deeds of those parlous times still live in memory, that Daniel Boone means much to the great Booneslick country which he and his intrepid companions snatched from the savages, can be impressed on the visitor in no more suitable way than by naming the big, modern fire-proof, metropolitan hotel after Daniel Boone.

And so two goals will be reached; the hotel, and a fitting monument to the pioneer who stamped his name on the history of the state and the country.

Miss Elizabeth Gentry of Kansas City, contributed to the new hotel a foot scraper, one foot tall, two feet wide, a relic of the old Selby Inn formerly located on the site of the Guitar building. Miss Gentry also gave an authentic picture of Daniel Boone. Miss Alta Gribble presented an oil painting of the house in St. Charles County in which Daniel Boone died.

Five years later a copy of Bingham's famous oil painting, which represents Daniel Boone's migration from North Carolina through the Cumberland Gap to Kentucky, was presented to the hotel. This was a magnificent copy, about six times as large as the original, very impressive, and the first in line of sight as guests entered the front door of the lobby.

* * *

In Praise of New J-School

Walter Williams, editor of the *Herald,* and Ed Watson, editor of the *Tribune,* were good friends and when Williams proposed to set up a Journalism School at M.U., Watson was supportive of the proposal. In an April 6, 1906 editorial Maverick, Ed wrote:

> *It's all right for our brethren of the country press to look at the attitude of the metropolitan press as they please, and the freedom of the press allows them to give utterance to their views, but the Tribune protests against them "knocking" the infant School of Journalism.*

Actually the Missouri School of Journalism began to operate as a school in September 1907, following a resolution made by the Board of Curators December 19,1906. On the same day, Editor Watson commented facetiously about his friend, Editor Williams:

> *We would like to say something about married men being in love with their wives, but we fear that Editor Williams has said all there is to say upon that subject.*

A few days later Watson commented on the Curator's resolution establishing a "college of journalism":

> *For several years the University has provided a series of lectures in journalism by men who have distinguished themselves in that field, but now it is proposed that a chair of journalism be developed, with a professor who is competent to train up young reporters and editors in the way they should go. The course is to be four years. Cornell* is the only other institution in the United States*

123

where newspaper men are made. It has been a successful
school of journalism on a grand scale.

Watson held up for the infant School of Journalism when he wrote:

There is a tendency among old-fashioned newspaper
men to sneer at colleges of journalism. Many people still
adhere to the ancient theory that journalists, like poets,
are born and not made, and to a certain extent that is
true, but even a newspaper man who has been "born"
can learn something if he is properly taught.

When Williams retired from active editorial control of the *Columbia Herald,* Ed wrote: "This means Mr. Williams has decided to accept the deanship of the school of journalism." In June 1908, an announcement was made that the student newspaper, the *Independent,* would be taken over by the School of Journalism and in its place would be published the *Daily Missourian.* Ed commented that students would be assigned as ad hustlers and as reporters. Students will be "sent on assignments and made to experience the practical work of daily newspaper production."

Three months later on September 1, 1908, Ed wrote:

Experience in gathering facts and writing them out in
readable style will be of value to every student who takes
the work offered by the department, whether the student
who takes the work, later becomes proprietor of a metro-
politan newspaper or not. The student's powers of ob-
seravation will necessarily increase with such practice.

Doubts About Missourian

On September 14, 1908, a *Tribune* headline announced that the *Missourian* Is Out Today. With that announcement "the fat was in the fire and the leopard revealed his spots." Ed began to wake up to the competitive possibilities presented by the infant *Missourian.* He wrote:

124

The Missourian has a liberal advertising patronage, and is in the field for such business as generally comes to a newspaper. It is submitted that this is competition. The state pays for the paper, the printing, and employs the publishers. If students were merely trained in journalism, there could be no possible objection to the Missourian, but in all fairness should the state go into the newspaper business against private individuals?

For the next twenty-nine years, Ed Watson treated the above theme in various forms of esoteric and vitriolic prose, but never in all those years did he indulge in personalities.

An editorial from Mitchell White's *Mexico Ledger* was reprinted in the *Tribune:*

The Ledger has always believed that a chair of journalism in Missouri University would not only add strength to the institution and prove of great benefit to the newspaper men of the state, but the management of the University Missourian should strenuously avoid competition with the local papers of Columbia. We feel confident that this will be the policy of Dean Williams and his associates.

Three days later on September 21, 1908 an editorial was reprinted in the *Tribune* from the *Hannibal Journal:*

The Journal agrees with the Moberly Democrat that the state University Daily, supported at state expense, should not be brought in competition with other Columbia newspapers. The School of Journalism is all right, but it ought to be conducted so as not to come in competition with private enterprise.

The Missouri legislature got into the act and attached a rider to a University appropriation bill, stipulating that "no part of the $854,000 appropriation shall be used for the publishing of a newspaper issued by the School of Journalism which received local paid advertising."

Not long after the first issue of the *Missourian* came out, an engineering student inadvertently became involved with the publication of the paper. Each day between ten and eleven o'clock, copy was taken to the Stephens Publishing Company from the Journalism School quarters in Switzler Hall. The Engineering School was next door to Switzler Hall, where *Missourian* copy was prepared, and it happened one morning that a journalism student asked his engineering friend to drop off the copy for the *Missourian* at the downtown publishing company at Broadway and Hitt Street.

The engineering student is presumed not to have known the necessity of getting the copy to the printers on time; or this may have been one of the pranks frequently perpetrated by engineers. Subsequently at about 1:30 p.m., the student arrived at the publishing plant, and as Ed commented, "was given a warm reception."

* * *

In July 1910, Walter Williams motored up the Booneslick Trail to gather material for historical articles. Upon his return he ventured the idea of marking the old road with suitable monuments through the state of Missouri. Watson concurred and wrote:

> The suggestion that Walter Williams made at the old Settlers meeting today that the old Booneslick Road should be perpetuated by markers and dragged, worked, and kept in first rate condition should be carried out. The old road was for a life time the principal artery of the commercial and social intercourse of Missouri, and its traditions and history should be fittingly preserved.

As of the year 1919, Watson retained friendship with Williams and, although he still thought the state did not belong in the newspaper business, he wrote a complimentary editorial on Williams as a Sunday School teacher.

> Dean Walter Williams is no more to be congratulated on the large attendance at the opening of his Sunday School

class than are those who have the opportunity to hear his instructive lectures on biblical subjects. Mr. Williams has travelled in the Holy Land and the lands adjacent to it and no man in America is better qualified to talk more learnedly than he.

Several years later in 1922, Ed wrote in his inimitable style, an editorial on THE JOYS OF JOURNALISM WEEK:

Each springtide "when lilies blow and clouds are highest up in the air," when a "lovelier iris changes on the burnished dove," we of Columbia experience the annual felicity of Journalism Week. It must be a joy indeed to those who are permitted each recurring year to journey to Columbia and drink deep from the Pierian spring of journalism that flows perennially in this quiet, uplifting atmosphere, perpetually and eternally in infinity and never ending joy where a part of the scheme which the Creator's infinite wisdom devised for this vale of tears. But the one sweetly solemn assurance that comes to us o'er and o'er is that while the light holds out to burn, this blessing will never become any less brighter by having taken its flight.

To be sure there are a few drawbacks to engaging in journalism in Columbia, but we assure those who might wish to share our privilege that they are merely minor matters of the bagatelle variety. For instance the great state of Missouri publishes a newspaper here in Columbia and one who strives to wrest a living from the same strenuous business must needs buck the resources of the sovereign commonwealth in which Columbia is located.

And then, visiting journalists, if perchance they have perspicacity and vision, and are canny and susceptible to the power of suggestion, may gain much valuable information regarding the art of how to get something for nothing. This information is not thrust upon the visiting journalist in any rough, unmannerly fashion, but rather is it left him to use his eyes and his gray matter.

The Tribune trusts that some of the visiting journalists, lured by the seductive joys of Journalism Week, may fold their tents at home and silently steal away to Columbia, there to enjoy every day of the year the real obsession of contentment and ease which the Tribune is forced to alone revel in. If this cordial, unselfish invitation is not accepted, the Tribune will be forced to continue to enjoy alone the distinction of being the only newspaper in America which competes with a sovereign state in the elevating business of journalism.

Some years prior to Williams becoming Dean of the School of Journalism, his speaking ability was greatly handicapped by a high, squeaky voice. A sudden and unexplained change came about, whereby his voice became deep and resonant. In remarking about this change, Ed wrote:

The delivery of Mr. Williams was a surprise to all. Since his change of voice, he has undoubted oratorical abilities. His intense, sincere and earnest manner, coupled with the things he has to say, has always made him a much sought after speaker. He has a bright future before him as an orator.

On November 18, 1934, three years before the death of Ed, Floyd C. Shoemaker, executive secretary of the State Historical Society of Missouri, wrote in a letter to Walter Williams: "I believe that Ed admires, respects and loves you, but of course, that does not include as yet one of your creations."*

Lynching

It Happened Here

The most traumatic story that Ed Watson edited during his more than forty years of newspapering was that of the lynching, Sunday morning, April 29, 1923, of a local man by members of a mob who were enraged because they believed the man had raped the 14-year-old daughter of a University of Missouri professor.

The alleged attack took place Friday, April 20, 1923, south of Stewart bridge, which crossed twenty-five feet above the Katy tracks at Stewart Road. The girl had been told by the attacker that a small child had wandered down the Katy tracks. The attacker then followed the girl after she had gone around the curve in the tracks, and soon caught up with her.

Seven days later the girl identified her attacker, and the next day again identified him, this time from her second-story window, when he was brought to her front yard. This was on Saturday and during the night there were groups of men on street corners, also gathered near the courthouse, angrily arguing that "something should be done."

That night the mob took the prisoner by force from the county jail and dragged him to Stewart bridge. By the time a rope strong enough to hang him was found, it was early Sunday morning. He was pushed from the bridge, protesting his innocence. A grand jury was called into session to investigate the lynching, but all five men who were charged and brought to trial, were found not guilty.

A similar lynching had taken place at Springfield, Mo., in 1906. Ed had been owner of the *Tribune* only three months, and he wrote:

The Springfield lynching is an awful blot on the fair name of our state. Every good citizen hopes that the leaders will be found and will be made examples of.

Seventeen years later, when the lynching took place in Columbia, as it had in Springfield, Ed was still for law and order. In speaking of several Columbia rapes that had happened within a two-week period, Watson said in an editorial: "These brutes and super-criminals should be dealt swift justice—by the courts, of course." Also, concerning rumors of mob action, he said: "Such people should be warned to let the law take its course."

Watson opposed those citizens of the town who tried to down-grade Columbia, and he maintained that it was a good and wholesome place to live. He particularly disagreed with nationally-known sociologist and chairman of the Sociology Department of the University, Dr. C.A. Ellwood, who was quoted in the *St. Louis Star* as declaring: "You cannot have a lynching unless a lot of people in the community believe in lynching." He further stated that the people of Columbia had "lower moral ideas" than the surrounding country.

The ire of Ed Watson was raised and he wrote:

While descanting on the moral degredation of Columbia, this savant and sociologist sees clearly what he regards as the mote in Columbia's eye, but is totally blind to the beam in his own—Columbia has this satisfaction: Dr. Ellwood has not qualified as an expert on fine drawn ethics and morals in the community which he calls home. The Doctor has eminently qualified as one of that variety of birds that despoils its own nest.

On the following day appeared a statement by Dr. Ellwood: "Owing to the vicious attack upon me through the editorial columns of the Daily Tribune and the attempt to belittle my reputation through false accusations and half truths, I am constrained to make a statement on my own behalf in order that the public may judge for itself whether or not such a slanderous editorial was justified."

130

Dr. Ellwood said that a student in one of his classes put words in his mouth and that he did not know that the student was a reporter for the *St. Louis Star.*

But Ed, unimpressed, wrote:

On the first page of today's Daily Tribune is a communication from Dr. C.A. Ellwood, professor of sociology in the University of Missouri, relative to statements, which a staff correspondent of the St. Louis Star, now in Columbia, sent to the Star. The Tribune yesterday printed what the Star's staff correspondent sent that paper: it again publishes the statement in order to compare it with Dr. Ellwood's communication in today's Tribune...Under the circumstances and the agreed statement of facts, the Tribune declines to make any apology whatsoever to Prof. Ellwood for the reason that none is due him. It thinks exactly as it did yesterday.

Friends

An Ankle Cure

Friends and the *Tribune* Family filled the days and many of the evening hours for Ed Watson. During the twenties when he suffered a slightly sprained ankle, he limped over to the Elk's Club on Tenth Street, just to the rear of the *Tribune* building, for consolation among his Elk Club brothers. The club's porter was solicitous and asked Colonel Watson if he could help in any way. Ed suggested that what he needed was some rubbing alcohol for his swollen ankle. The porter soon returned, and suggested to the Colonel that "it was a terrible waste of alcohol." He thought the ankle could be cured without all that waste. Ed gave his permission, and the porter returned with a punch bowl, some grape juice, oranges and other ingredients, including grain alcohol. This was going to be such a fine cure for the ankle that Ed decided to call up his downtown business friends,* invite them to the club and all could celebrate his "birthday." Ed Watson had frequent "birthdays"—whenever he wanted to have his friends in. This party was an enjoyable occasion, and very shortly Ed's ankle was cured.

Fount of Wisdom and Knowledge

A good friend to scores of people, Ed Watson was also admired by many acquaintances. Nelle Kitchens, former mathematics teacher at Columbia High School for thirty-five years, recalled that Colonel Ed was the "fount of wisdom and knowledge." "When anyone wanted to know anything about anything, they sought out the Colonel, who invariably had the answer," she said.

Proponent of Free Speech

One of Ed's first downtown luncheon partners was Father C.E. Byrne, pastor of Sacred Heart Catholic Church, who later became Bishop of Galveston, Texas. On one occasion, Father Byrne brought up the subject of an article, appearing in the *Columbia Herald,* which he thought needed answering. It was reported that a local pastor had said in his previous Sunday sermon that the next war in this country would be between Protestants and Catholics.

Father Byrne wanted to answer the charge, and sought Ed's advice. Ed, who at the time was Columbia City Attorney, deplored the idea of a fight between Protestants and Catholics, but maintained the Protestant minister's right to free speech. He also thought that Father Byrne had the right to challenge the minister's statement and he arranged with the *Herald* for the priest's answer to be published.

* * *

A Speakeasy Tale

During prohibition days, Watson and some friends drove to St. Louis on a business trip. When they arrived in the city, they stopped at a speakeasy, called the Round House. Three of Ed's friends were his contemporaries, including Stark Dorsey, druggist; John Platt, electrician; and R.W. Wright, a sheet metal man. The fourth was young Bill Hulett, who worked for Wright in the sheet metal business.

After several bottles of home brew were consumed, tongues were loosened and all were on a first name basis, including young Bill Hulett. Bill tells the story: "I was getting quite friendly with Mr. Watson, calling him 'Ed'—just like the older men,

SANDERS-Co. ST. L

After several years climbing steep steps to put out the *Tribune* at the Whittle building, Ed Watson decided it was time to establish his newspaper on the first floor. In 1909 he made plans with Judge J.A. Stewart to occupy the ground floor of the building Stewart was to build at the northwest corner of Broadway and North Seventh Street. Watson had ordered the new press and it was ready to be shipped. But Stewart was slower getting the building up than promised. Consequently Watson made arrangements to move into a building known as the Nowell annex, a small building south of the new three-story W.B. Nowell building, occupied on the ground floor by Nowell's Grocery. The latter building has been lowered to one story and is now owned by Acacia Lodge, A.F. & A.M. The *Tribune's* annex is now occupied by the Potion Parlor and The Bookseller.

On February 12, 1921 the *Tribune* moved its operations into its own new building at the northeast corner of Ninth and Locust streets, now occupied by Mister Guy—Clothiers, and the Logos Book Store.

whom he had known all his life. After several times of 'Ed this and Ed that,' Mr. Watson said: 'Young man, I think I'd better know your first name—you seem to know mine pretty well.'"

Young Bill Hulett's father, W.B. "Bill" Hulett, also a good friend of Ed's was in the cab business during the early 1900's. He had been asked by Ed to pick up Margaret Waters, Ed's sister, who was to leave for Kansas City. The Wabash was scheduled to leave next morning at 9:00 o'clock, and he asked Bill to set 8:30 for the cab's arrival time at the Dean Waters home on the College of Agriculture campus.

On the following morning, 8:30 arrived, then it was 8:45 and finally 9:00, but the clop-clop of horses drawing a hack could not be heard, and Ed was upset. By this time, the train had pulled out and Mrs. Waters decided there was nothing to do but leave on the following morning. Ed agreed that he would go to the cab office next morning. He wanted to give Bill a piece of his mind and he would also make sure there was no further slip up. He was still upset when he walked into the cab office about 8:00 o'clock the next morning.

Bill was there and knew he was in for trouble. Before Ed could say anything, Bill blurted out: "Ed, the reason I didn't pick up your sister yesterday, I was drunk."

Knowing a good excuse when he heard one, Ed replied: "That's all right, Bill, why didn't you say so."

* * *

A Social Highball

Young Dot Sappington, who was to be the founder of Central Dairy, was fond of telling about an incident involving him and the older Watson. When he was employed by the White Eagle Dairy,* it became necessary for him to go to work quite early in order to check out the milk wagons. One morning someone knocked on the locked front door. He saw that it was Colonel Ed Watson, and he immediately admitted him. Mr. Watson

135

asked if he had some crushed ice: "If you'll get the ice, I'll furnish the highball, and we'll have a drink together." This suited Dot fine, and the two enjoyed their highballs.

On the following morning Colonel Watson was at the door again, and this continued for several mornings until Dot reconsidered his situation. He was working for another man, and also was rearing seven children; maybe it would be best if he called a halt to the morning drink.

Next morning Colonel Ed knocked at the door. Dot let him in and said: "Colonel Watson, I'll be glad to get you the crushed ice, but I have a family to support, and I'd better not drink any more, as much as I enjoy it." The Colonel replied: "Oh well, I don't want to drink alone." And he walked away.

* * *

Gentleman and Scholar

Mary Paxton Keeley, Missouri's first woman Journalism School graduate, class of 1910, described Colonel Ed as a "gentleman and a scholar." She said that she and Ruth Prather Midyette, both widows, "went to various functions, picnics and the like, with the Colonel. Ruth called him 'Mr. Ed' but I stuck with 'Colonel Ed'".

A future Washington correspondent for the *St. Louis Post-Dispatch,* Charles G. Ross, with whom Mary Paxton was at one time engaged to be married, was a good friend of Ed Watson, although some years younger. "Charles' mother prevented her son from getting married," Mary said, "because she had a sizable family and needed Charlie's financial aid." Subsequently they both were married, Mary Paxton to Edmund Keeley, and Charlie Ross to Miss Florence Griffin.

"Colonel Ed was engaged to be married," Mary Paxton continued, "to a girl who had gone to Stephens College, and whose home was in Chicago. This engagement was broken off, and the girl later married a Chicago man, who lived only a few years. Colonel Ed was a one-woman man," said Mrs. Keeley,

After Watson's death on November 30, 1937 Henry Jackson
"Jack" Waters Jr., took over management of the *Tribune*. On
July 19, 1947 he moved the *Tribune* into its new home at the
northeast corner of South Seventh and Cherry streets. A second
floor was added to the east end of the building in 1960.

Above picture was taken May 25, 1966 when Jack Waters announced his retirement from active supervision of the paper. His
son, Henry Jackson "Hank" Waters III succeeded him. Hank
had joined the *Tribune* staff in 1948 and became Advertising
Manager in 1959.

Plans for the present *Tribune* building began in 1967 and in
April, 1972 construction started. The new *Tribune* building at
101 North Fourth Street was occupied December 10, 1973.

"and you could say he was disappointed in love."

In respect to the friendship between Watson and Walter Williams, Mrs. Keeley said: "Colonel Ed didn't like the *Missourian,* but he and Walter were good friends. Following the second marriage of Williams to Sara Lockwood, many of Walter's friends were 'weaned away' by Sara, who was jealous of his friends, both men and women."

That Was No Bum

Shortly after Frank St. Clair and his new bride, Mary Agnes Booth, were married, they were returning from viewing a show at the recently opened Missouri Theatre. Upon arriving at their parked car, Frank discovered that his car ignition key was missing. He retraced his steps to the theatre and asked employees for a search of the premises, but the search was fruitless. The car was parked at the side of the *Tribune* building, South Ninth and Locust streets, and Frank decided to inquire of someone moving about inside the office as to whether or not the key had been found and turned in to the office.

The key had not been turned in, but Frank returned with the *Tribune's* panel truck key. Mrs. St. Clair asked the identity of "the bum" that Frank had been talking to, and as Frank turned on the ignition to the truck, he replied: "That was no bum, Mary. That was the generous owner of the *Tribune,* Ed Watson, who is making it possible for you and I to get home tonight."

Ed Watson, big and impressive looking on occasion, could be as "plain as a shoe" when he got into his fox hunting clothes.

* * *

Knights of the Road

Tramps, including tramp printers, frequently came to the *Tribune* for newspapers that they used to wrap around themselves inside their clothes as insulation material for warmth. Invariably Ed Watson took time off his work to talk to these Knights of the Road. "You get good information and insights by talking to them," he said.

Watson maintained a meal ticket at Morris' Restaurant, and with a note from himself to Freda Morris, any tramp could get a good meal. Ed often went with the man and sat at the table to talk to him. He never gave money to tramps because he knew they would squander it on drink when they needed food.

One such tramp, a very sick man, was taken by Watson in a cab to the Boone County Hospital. The next day when he went to see the man and to arrange for paying his hospital bill, he found that he had died of lockjaw. Hospital authorities had gotten the man's name and had notified his relatives.

Another weary Willie, as Watson called him, claimed a Harvard education and had "beaten" his way inland to see this "Athens of Missouri." Branch railroads were usually too hard to "beat." But this wanderer had "perambulated into town." Watson commented editorially:

> He was practically sans shoes and sans sartorial adornment of any kind, a picturesque type. He plied his calling as other tramps do until he was taken in charge of by the night watchman, Joseph Bauman, and placed in the calaboose as a guest of Michael Tyson, keeper of the city bastile. There was no charge against him but he was put in to insure him keeping out of mischief. He said his name was not John Doe, but that cognoman would do. His patronymic, he said, was well known and it might make his forebears blush if they knew he was drilling around the country as a tramp and the guest in holdovers.

> John Doe said he was a graduate of Harvard College and had bright prospects in New York as a lawyer. Dope and booze, as he expressed it, had been his undoing and he finally became a knight of the road.

> "I leaned a little toward matters and things intellectual," he said, "and I knew that the State University was located here. The old columns impressed me more than anything

138

else. They are beautiful and there is nothing at any East-
ern college that I have seen that compares with them in
classic lines."

Doe talked certainly of other things and showed that his
claims to one-time refinement were well made. He was
given hours to leave town and availed himself of the op-
portunity after being released from the calaboose this
morning.

Ed's newspaper friend, Kelly Pool, editor of the *Centralia Courier*, hired a tramp printer who worked for Pool several months, "the best printer I ever had," he said. "Then one day someone called me to let me know my printer had forged my name to a Ten Dollar check. I looked around for awhile for the man, but he was gone—probably went back to Chicago—with my Ten Dollars."

Not all tramps, however, were dishonest. Ed frequently commented that he trusted tramps as much as he trusted others, and more than he trusted millionnaires.

"It seems that the rich are never sent to prison," he wrote. "Some way or other there is some technicality through which they escape. But how different with the poor man, especially the cheap criminal who steals things of little value."

Calling on his experience as a reporter in St. Louis and in Ft. Worth, Texas, he said:

Any police reporter in a city can tell how such a one is
treated. They can't tell about the sweat box; they don't
know what happens there, but it is not an uncommon
thing for a desk-sergeant to mistreat a prisoner who re-
fused to talk. But the men who steal millions are some-
how or other protected by the law. When they are caught
and convicted, they are not sent to prison. The court of
appeals or the supreme court finds something wrong,
and in the end the man is free.

Ed also cited the case of the peddler who came to town. While walking through the University campus, he found a pock-etbook containing a twenty dollar bill and a half dollar. University Librarian W.K. Stone advised him to advertise for the owner in the *Tribune,* and then notified Ed that the man would be in to see him.

The one-armed man found the *Tribune,* gave the ad to Watson, but could leave no address, so he asked the location of the priest in town and said he would leave the pocketbook with the pastor of the local Catholic church.

Later Father Arthur Pleuss told Watson that he had fed the man before he went on his way, leaving the Twenty Dollars and the half dollar behind to await the results of the ad. Next day, following publication of the ad, a young lady came into the *Tribune* office, described the pocketbook, what was in it, and Ed made the call to Father Pleuss so that the property could be returned to the owner. Ed's comment was that since the man was selling shoe strings and corn cures, he hoped his readers "would purchase some of his wares, if they chanced to see him, no matter whether you are the possessor of many shoe strings, or not the possessor of a single corn, for he is one among a thousand."

* * *

George's First Customer

Late in life a friend of Ed's was George Brake, an immegrant from Greece, who opened a hat-blocking and tux-rental shop in 1933, the middle year of the Great Depression. Brake put a small ad in the *Tribune* to announce his opening at 23 S. Ninth Street. On the next morning Ed came in the front door of the new business with three hats to be cleaned and blocked. He was George's first customer.

* * *

A Nephew's Assessment

Berry Allen Watson, named for his grandfather, Dr. Watson, was a nephew of Ed's who attended the University and worked as a reporter for the *Tribune*. Berry described his uncle as "a brilliant loner, whose passion was for truth and knowledge. He read hundreds of books and imparted part of what he read through his editorials. He felt more comfortable with his first love, newspapering, and left his law career for it. He and his life-long confidante, James Moss, were 'printer's devils' together at the old *Columbia Herald* when they were teen-agers."

The *Tribune* office was only a couple of blocks from the home of Berry's parents—Laws and Jean Watson—on Watson Place, and in his last years, Ed partially deserted the boarding houses and restaurants, taking his evening meal in the home of his brother.

* * *

A Birthday Celebration

At the approach of Watson's sixty-fifth birthday anniversary on November 29, 1932, some of the newspaper's employees decided to have a surprise celebration for him. A dinner at the Daniel Boone Tavern, where he had resided for twelve years, was planned for *Tribune* employees only. But when some of Ed's friends outside the newspaper heard of the plans, they expressed a desire to share in the event. It was left to nephew Jack Waters to inveigle Uncle Ed into being present at the hotel. A large, two-tiered cake was provided by hotel owner, Frank Leonard. The dinner was attended by sixty-five friends and employees. The surprise was complete. Ed closed the celebration by acknowledging the compliment to him by his friends, and the next day expressed his thanks in an editorial titled: "An Appreciation."

To individuals "friendship's the wine of life"; to a newspaper it's that intangible asset defined as "good will," without which the life of a newspaper is apt to be brief and unprofitable—in no way a satisfaction or a gratification to its publishers, nor a benefit to the community it should seek to serve. Like wine, friendship is exhilarating and a delight to those who are so fortunate as to be its recipient. But the fruit of friendship is perennial and lasting, in contrast to the effervescence of the fruit of the vine.

The editor of the Tribune last evening had occasion to appreciate and realize the significance and import of friendship when he was the guest of honor at the Daniel Boone Tavern at a surprise dinner tendered by sixty-five friends celebrating his sixty-fifth birthday anniversary. It was the most joyous, the most gratifying, the red-letter occasion of all the sixty-one and a half years Columbia has been his home. Words are poor vehicles to express the gratitude, the appreciation, the deep emotion which last night's token engendered. It was flowers for the living, and the donors of the inestimable offering of invaluable friendship may be assured that last evening's happy event will live longest and greenest in the memory of him, and all the dinner signified and means to the Tribune and him.

* * *

Where's John L. Lewis?

Two years before Watson died, there was much labor union activity all over the country, and when the composing room employees went on strike, Ed was in Chicago. He arrived home the next day after the strike began, and he hurried to the office. His red cheeks were puffed out, and he was perspiring.

"Where is John L. Lewis?" he shouted as he walked through the doorway. John L. Lewis was not there, but an International Typographical Union officer had come in and convinced the men to vote a strike. To most of those who struck, this was a sad day, because "the Boss had always treated his employees as family."

Three Score and Ten

When Watson first took over the *Tribune* he had just reached the age of thirty-eight. In one of his early Maverick columns he commented on age:

'Tis laughable to hear some blase chap of thirty, talking about how old he is getting. Why, you haven't time to begin to think about how old in your alloted three score and ten, as long as you live in this jewel box of a world of ours, along with these wonderful fairies called 'men.'

Ed's mention of "three score and ten" may be taken as a prophecy.

Last Respects to Bodine

Tom Bodine, editor of the *Paris (Mo.) Mercury,* preceded in death by four months his good friend, Ed Watson. Bodine had asked that his body be "laid in state" in the *Mercury* office, where he had spent so much of his life. He asked that the flat bed press be run, and that his casket be open so that his friends could "pay their last respects."

Editor Bodine, who died on Thursday, July 29, 1937, had written the week before that "The Paris Mercury is being edited this week and may be edited next week by Mr. Paul Alexander, a former employee and known to the readers throughout Monroe County. He is of the Ed Watson type of newspaperman, and wields a wicked pen, and the readers of the Mercury will not find him lacking in anything from high court editorials to fox hounds."

Bodine and Watson had been honored years before by the

Missouri State Medical Society which elected them Honorary Life members, though neither man was a physician and neither had studied to be one. The two men, so much alike in their mode of life and chosen profession, were close friends. Both men were excellent writers, hard-hitting with their editorials, devoted to the profession of journalism, independent in thought and completely honest. Neither man had married, and both were able to spend more time on the job than their married counterparts.

An unusual method of writing an editorial was practiced by Bodine, who sat on a stool at the type case, and letter by letter, selected each piece of type to form his editorial, without first writing it out either on a typewriter or by long hand.

The old well-worn stool and typecase were at the foot of Bodine's casket and Ed Watson remarked that he "preferred his old stub pencil to the typecase." But Watson appreciated Bodine's method because he, too, had learned the case and how to hand-set type at the *Columbia Herald.*

* * *

Another newspaper friend of Ed's was found dead in an adjoining county boardinghouse where he lived. Like Watson the friend had been a bachelor. Both gave their lives to newspapering. The friend's life mirrored the life of Ed, himself. And the *Tribune* editor wrote of him in terms that easily could have been applied to himself:

He was unfortunate in being addicted to the use of liquor to excess, but was always treated with consideration by his brother newspapermen, because of his gentlemanly bearing when sober and on account of his unusual ability. He was a writer of far above the average ability, and could have had employement on the best newspapers in the country had it not been for his disposition. As a writer of verse, he had few equals in the West. Newspapermen

144

all over Missouri, who esteemed him highly when he was his real self, will sincerely regret his untimely passing.

* * *

"When Mr. Watson died," said Mrs. Irma North, a former *Tribune* employee, "I had not worked at the newspaper long. My father had died a short time before, and on the first day of my return to the office, following the funeral of my father, Mr. Watson walked straight over to me and said: 'I'm sorry,' and turned and shuffled away. He said it so kindly and sincerely, that I almost broke down and cried. I've always remembered this about him. The gesture itself was so meaningful that I've remembered it for my own usage in making a response to grief.

* * *

Last Editorial

In Ed Watson's last editorial Saturday morning, November 13, 1937, he castigated two Democratic political organizations, Tammany of New York and Pendergast of Kansas City. Accompanying his editorial was a *Christian Science Monitor* feature story citing the evils of Tammany Hall, and praising the voters for rising up against it. Watson editorialized:

On this page is some "good readin" for every citizen, man or woman, resident of burg or metropolis, if interested in good and honest local government. Especially is this true of government in large cities, where there is more inclination, and more opportunity for vicious political practices, greater development for a desire to live without labor or effort of any kind and become a moocher, a barnacle, a tax eater of taxes paid by the public. Delectable and interesting and informing to a degree should the story be to residents of Kansas City, for it tells accurately a tale of how Tammany, corrupt, vicious, impregnable, political organization which paraded for decades that won control of the municipal affairs of New York City in the guise of democracy and with the label of the party name, minus every vestige of principle or of honest intent. The story is also an enlightening and informing tale of how the people, tiring of political corruption and crime, finally became sufficiently outraged to rise in their might and bring the man-eating Tiger to heel—in fact toss his carcass clean and clear of the bailiwick. Public sentiment was the bouncer.

So vicious and corruptible was Tammany in its most flourishing and palmiest days, it has never had a thing on the so-called Democratic organization in Kansas City, labelled the Pendergast machine but dripping with Republicans or any seekers after public pap or the patronage trough. Columnists and foreign commentators and delvers into the seamy side of American politics, almost unhesitatingly place the crown of iniquity on the brow of the Kansas City organization—in other words, long odds could safely be laid on the Metropolis of Kaw methods as the bellwether of unopposed political corruption.

The story on this page tells how the Tiger's lashing tail was amputated at the root, his fangs drawn, and his claws chiseled off with the power of public sentiment.

Kansas City or any other metropolis or any municipality of any size or kind can take many leaves out of New York's experiences in the last two city elections and elect and install whatever kind of public officials they desire— honest or corrupt. If the people of Kansas City want to turn thumbs down on the corrupt administration of public affairs they have been receiving, lying supine and timorous, they have the power to throw the offenders out by the scruff of their necks. If they do not, the majority of the voting citizenry falls within the Pendergast organization and subscribes to its standards and political tenets.

"30"

On the day of this editorial, which shows his usual fire, Ed Watson attended Homecoming activities at the University and spent some time Sunday morning at his office, but by evening he was feeling ill and was taken to the Boone County Hospital, where he was pronounced as having had a heart attack. Later it was announced that he had a cerebral hemmorhage and was in serious condition. He rallied some but finally signed "30" to a full life of newspapering on the day following his seventieth birthday, November 30, 1937.*

Edwin Moss Watson had reached his "three score and ten." This was the allotted time his mother had asked for her son in a poem she sent to him on his twenty-sixth birthday in 1893 at Ft. Worth, Texas, and titled:

A BIRTHDAY POEM

I won't send any pudding
Nor I won't send any pie,
For if I did, dear child,
You might eat too much and die.

But for this birthday cake
Don't fail due thanks to give,
And ask the kind good Father
That you may eat and live.

I, too, will ask that you may live
For three score and ten,
And may I live to see you
A man amid good men.

Notes

Page 1

The title "Colonel" was used in Ed Watson's time as a sign of respect and honor for an individual. There need be no connection with the military to be so-designated, and just about anyone could hold the title. Col. Watson came by it "more or less honestly," as he said, when Gov. Guy B. Park selected him for the Governor's staff of Honorary Colonels.

Page 2

Mission School, located at the northeast corner of Hinkson Avenue and North William Street, was one of the early schools established in Columbia—always a school town. It was a "subscription" school, built by J.L. Stephens, pioneer merchant and father of E.W. Stephens. Another school that Edwin attended following his years at Mission School was Baptist Female Academy, which had been renamed and officially designated in the upper classes as Stephens Female College. This school was also supported by J.L. Stephens and was named in his honor in October 1870. Later in 1917 the "Female" designation was dropped and the school became the now nationally known Stephens College.

Page 2

Flat Branch now runs sluggishly underground through concrete storm drains on the east side of Providence Road. It has its beginning east of the Wabash tracks near Park Avenue. It parallels Park Avenue, running beneath the street. When it comes to Providence Road, it bends south, still unseen underground. It crosses under Broadway at Providence Road and parallels the Katy road bed until it reaches Hinkson Creek.

Page 3
Two of the servants rest in the Watson family plot in Columbia Cemetery—Joe Taylor, "Faithful Servant, 77 Yrs Old," and Mahala Taylor, "Faithful Servant, 45 Yrs Old."

Page 3
The Old Spring, also known as the Chalybeate Spring, was believed to have medicinal qualities. In 1916 Ed urged the University to unclog the spring, erect a pagoda and make the spring water available to students and townspeople once more. The spring was located on the west side of Ninth Street. Its water flowed into Goose Creek and under what later was known as the "Kissing Bridge" on the Journalism School campus.

Page 9
Old Academic Hall burned down on January 9, 1892 leaving the present day columns on Francis Quadrangle.

Page 9
The Stephens home was located south of what is now Stephens College Stables. Present day Windsor Street, if extended, would run into the housesite. The house stood on a hill facing south, overlooking what is now Walnut Street.

Page 10
Mattie Watson was the first death in the Watson family. She died January 22, 1882, age 10 years.

Page 15
Touchdowns accounted for 4 points; field goals were worth 2 points.

Page 16
The "Anderson home" was in reality the Watson home on South Ninth Street. Mrs. Watson was fond of Sam and depended on him to find her son, Edwin, when she needed him. Sam knew all the campus hangouts and where to look for Ed, on the latter's visits home.

Page 17
The "small boy" was Ed's youngest brother, Carson, who during Sam's playing years from 1891 to 1894 was between nine and twelve years old.

Page 19
Watson always referred to himself as proprietor instead of publisher.

Page 20
The location of the *Tribune* when Watson took it over was in the Whittle building, 903A Broadway, a second story location, now occupied by the Kai Min Restaurant.

Page 20
One of Central Hotel's walls, before the building burned November 29, 1910, abutted the brick wall that is now the west wall of Commerce Bank, Sixth and Broadway; the Gordon Hotel is now the Niedermeyer Apartments, Cherry and South Tenth

streets; the Athens Hotel is now the Wabash Apartments, Walnut and North Ninth streets; the Powers House was also destroyed by fire and is now the location of the Parker Funeral Home, Tenth and Walnut streets.

Page 21
Kings Highway was later paved with brick and renamed Stewart Road.

Page 33
Old Columbia High School now the location of Jefferson Junior High School, North Eighth and Rogers streets.

Page 34
The Fyfer building that was constructed with bricks from the old courthouse was located at the southeast corner of Broadway and Hitt Street. The two top floors were removed from the building and the one floor is now occupied by Campus Cinema Theatres.

Page 34
Pronounced Pay-quin, not Paa-quin. Paquin Street was named for the Paquin family, two members of which were Dr. Ozias Paquin and Dr. Paul Paquin.

Page 36
The Hamilton-Brown Shoe factory that began operations in 1907 closed its doors during the Great Depression when so many businesses throughout the country failed in the 1930's. Today the building houses Atkins Chemical and Services Co., Wilkes Boulevard and Fay Street.

Page 39
Water Street, bordering Flat Branch on the east, is now Fourth Street.

Page 39
George McManus, creator of the "Maggie & Jiggs" comic strip, was a friend of Ed Watson.

Page 49
Terrapin Neck is a strip of land on both sides of the Huntsdale Bottoms, extending northwest toward Rocheport and southeast almost to Providence. It later extended to the hills on both sides of Terrapin Creek, and other hills around Huntsdale.

Page 52
Brushwood Lake is reached by the Katy roadbed, about two miles north of McBaine.

Page 61
On the death of Ed Watson in 1937, his nephew H.J. "Jack" Waters Jr., took over the *Tribune,* and continued its operation until 1966 when Jack's son, Henry J. "Hank" Waters III, was given the reins.

Page 62
"Hearne is a fictitious name; the incident is factual.

Page 63
Subscribers to the *Tribune* knew that when the editor wrote that

"the *Tribune* said this or that'" it clearly meant that "Ed Watson said this or that." There also was an occasional editorial "we" but usually when anything was said it was the *Tribune* that did the saying.

Page 74
"Jay School," at one time commonly written for "Journalism School." Today more common usage is "J-School."

Page 78
Stone's Music Hall was the location of the *Tribune* when it published its first issue, September 12, 1901. The north end of the hall had a third floor, a kind of a gallery room over-looking the high-ceilinged ballroom. Two flights of stairs had to be climbed by young C.M. Strong, publisher, to reach the third floor, and after arriving, he found space very cramped but it was all that he could afford.

Page 84
Morris' Restaurant, 15 S. Ninth St., was owned and managed by Jim and Freda Morris. "Mr. Watson was like a member of the family," Freda Morris said. "He had his own reserved table, and requested that we provide him with his own linen napkin. Jim always had charge of Mr. Watson's meal ticket and made sure that the ticket was punched only by himself."

Page 123
The controversy over whether or not the University of Missouri School of Journalism is the oldest in the world is one of semantics. The words "schools" and "departments" are the key words, and Missourians contend that we have the first "school." Ed Watson spoke of Cornell University as having "a successful

school of Journalism on a grand scale." But modern day historians from Cornell claim only to have had a "department" of journalism prior to the founding of the School of Journalism at the University of Missouri.

Page 128
By "one of your creations," Shoemaker was referring to the *Missourian.*

Page 133
Friends frequently heard Ed comment on inflation as he proclaimed that "good, Kentucky, Bourbon whiskey can never be priced too high. "

Page 135
The White Eagle Dairy was located on South Tenth Street, between Broadway and Cherry Street, now occupied by Wayland Office Supply Company. Later the dairy moved to the corner of South Eighth and Locust streets, to a new building, now the location of Kelly Press.

Page 147
On Thursday, December 3, 1937, the day Edwin Moss Watson was buried, all business in downtown Columbia stopped for five minutes. The funeral filled the First Baptist Church at Broadway and Waugh Street and hundreds stood outside. As the funeral procession filed by on Broadway to Columbia Cemetery, all cars on cross streets stopped and pedestrians stood quietly.

Watson Chronology

November 29, 1867

Edwin Moss Watson, second child of the Dr. B.A. Watson family of six children, was born at Millersburg. His older sister, Eugenia Estelle "Stella" Watson, was born in Williamsburg, Mo., on March 18, 1866.

October 10, 1869

Margaret, the third Watson child, was born at Millersburg.

January 8, 1872

Martha Allen "Mattie" Watson, the fourth Watson child, was born in Millersburg.

Summer, 1872

Dr. B.A. Watson family moved to Columbia. Edwin was four and one-half years old.

September, 1873

Edwin and Stella to Mission School, Hinkson Avenue and William Street.

1876

Dr. Watson bought Warren Woodson plantation house on South Ninth and Elm streets.

June 11, 1876

Samuel Laws, the fifth Watson child, was born; died April 21, 1942, age 66 years.

September, 1879

Edwin to Baptist School—later renamed Stephens College.

1881-1890

Ed worked for E.W. Stephens, starting as a printer's devil on the *Columbia Herald,* and continuing with the *Herald* until his graduation from M.U. in 1890.

December 12,1881

Carson, the sixth Watson child, was born.

January 22, 1882

Martha Allen "Mattie" Watson died, age 10 years.

September, 1885

Entered Arts & Science College at M.U.

June, 1890

Received A.B. degree from M.U.

1890-1891

Reporter on *St. Joseph Ballot.*

January 9, 1892

Academic hall fire (six columns remain).

August 25, 1892-1894

Reporter on *Fort Worth Star-Telegram.*

1894 to 1896

Studied law at M.U.--obtained J.D. degree.

1895

Future brother-in-law Dr. H.J. Waters returned to M.U. as dean of the college of agriculture.

January 14, 1896

Carson Watson died, age 14 years.

June, 1897

Margaret Watson wed to Dean H.J. Waters.

1897-1898

Ed elected Columbia City Attorney; joined Wellington Gordon law firm; served one year as city attorney.

1899-1901

Ed was editor of the *Jefferson City State Tribune.*

June 3, 1900

H.J. "Jack" Waters Jr. born in Columbia.

1901-1905

Ed worked as reporter for the *St. Louis Star* and the *St. Louis Republic.*

1902

Outbuildings of Woodson plantation house were torn down in readiness for subdividing. A new street, Watson Place, was surveyed.

November 29, 1905

E.L. Mitchell, owner of *Tribune* died.

December 15, 1905

Ed Watson announced as the new editor and proprietor of the *Columbia Daily Tribune*, then located at 911A Broadway in the Whittle Building, now occupied by Kai Min restaurant.

January 10, 1906

Dan McFarland became City Editor

June 27, 1906

Walter Chester, who had been Mitchell's business manager went to a newspaper in Okmulgee, Okla.

February 1906

Dr. Watson's lots for sale on Watson Place.

March 12, 1906

Dr. Waters was Acting M.U. President.

August 25, 1906

Dr. Watson built home on Watson Place.

October 6, 1906

Tribune moved across hall at Whittle Building to a location at the right of the stairs, now occupied by KOPN radio station.

December 19, 1906

M.U. School of Journalism established.

February 8, 1908

University Missourian established by legislature.

September 14, 1908

First issue of *University Missourian*.

May 8, 1908

Robert W. "Bob" Jones became city editor of the *Tribune*.

June 19, 1909

Dean H.J. Waters to Kansas State University as President.

November 29, 1910

Tribune moved to Nowell Annex, 23 N. Ninth Street.

September 18, 1911

Hollis Edwards became City Editor of the *Tribune*.

September 1, 1915

Stella died, age 49 years.

January 19, 1918

Dr. Watson died.

1919

M.D. Jett and J.P. Hamel to *Tribune*.

February 12, 1921

Tribune moved to new building at Ninth and Locust streets.

1924

H.J. "Jack" Waters Jr. to *Tribune*.

October 26, 1925

Dr. H.J. Waters Sr. died.

April 22, 1927

Clara Watson died.

June 7, 1930

H.J. "Hank" Waters III born.

November 30, 1937

Edwin Moss Watson died.

Tribune Chronology

September 12, 1901

The *Columbia Daily Tribune* was founded by Charles Munro Strong, a young man just graduated from the University of Missouri, who had a few spare dollars to gamble. His mentor in the scheme was an experienced printer, Charles G. Duncan, whose primary claim to fame was that he "knew the complete works of Shakespeare by heart."

September 17, 1901

The two men were joined five days later by Barrett O'Hara, M.U. graduate, who later was elected Lieutenant-Governor of Illinois. The three men did all the *Tribune* work on the third floor of Stone's Music Hall at 15 South Ninth Street. The first floor is now occupied by Uncle Sam's, Safari Outfitters, and is a one-story building. The two top floors were lopped off at the same time that the city's new parking building to the rear was erected.

September 16, 1902

Ernest L. Mitchell brought some much needed capital—his wife's—to the *Tribune* when he became a partner of Strong's.

September 18, 1902

Two days following the forming of the new partnership between Mitchell and Strong, the *Tribune's* operations were moved to the second floor of the Whittle Building, 911A Broadway, now the location of the Kai Min Restaurant.

January 28, 1905

C.M. Strong sold his interest in the *Tribune* to Mitchell to become public relations manager and advance man for Morton Pemberton, the well-known Boone County-born humorist who was billed throughout the country as "Reuben." At this time, Shannon Mountjoy, grandson of University of Missouri President James Shannon, was writing most of the *Tribune* editorials under the philosophical heading of "The Things of This World." Later he was to make a name for himself in Oklahoma journalism.

September 3, 1905

Ernest Mitchell became ill, his illness being diagnosed as typhoid. For the next three months he was confined to his home, lingering in illness until his death November 29, 1905—Ed Watson's birthday. When Mitchell died, Watson was a reporter for the *St. Louis Republic.* He was on vacation somewhere in the Caribbean, sailing with a friend who owned a yacht. But it was well-known to members of his family that he wanted to own a newspaper. Mitchell's widow was a personal friend of Ed's sister, Margaret Waters, who solicited the aid of her husband, Dr. H.J. Waters, then Dean of the University of Missouri College of Agriculture, and of her father, Dr. B.A. Watson. Between the two men a loan of $3,000, Mrs. Mitchell's asking price for the paper, was arranged at the Exchange National Bank.

December 15, 1905

When Watson returned from his cruise, he took over $1,000 of the note, and the newspaper. He listed himself next day as "Editor and Proprietor." This was the beginning of the Watson and Waters family connection with the paper.

October 6, 1905

The *Tribune* moved across the hall at the Whittle building to the rooms now occupied by KOPN Radio Station.

November 29, 1910

The *Tribune* moved to the Nowell Annex, 23 N. Ninth Street, now occupied by two businesses, the Potion Parlor and The Bookseller. The W.B. Nowell Grocery building next door on the southwest corner of Ninth and Walnut streets, was a three story building, now lowered to one story and owned by Acacia Lodge, A.F. & A.M.

February 12, 1921

The *Tribune* moved into its own new building at Ninth and Locust streets, now occupied by Mister Guy, clothiers, and by Logos Book Store.

July 19, 1947

The *Tribune* moved to sixth location, a building at the corner of Seventh and Cherry streets, now occupied by Deja Vu night club.

December 10, 1973

A new *Tribune* building was completed and occupied at 101 North Fourth Street. Plans for the building began in 1967 and in April 1972 construction started. The printing process had progressively advanced from early hand type-setting methods of 1901 to the present, modern, computerized photocomposition system. The new offset press has a capacity to print a 64-page paper.

Acknowledgements

Grateful acknowledgment is given to the following people for their contributions to this book: Sam Anderson, Opal (Ward) Ashlock, Paul Bell, Dr. G.A. Bradford, George Brake, Wendell H. Crow, Clyde H. Duncan, Harold Duncan, James Garth, James W. Goodrich, Leonard Guitar, Jack Hackethorn, Fred Hatton, Oler Hombs, G.W. "Bill" Hulett, M.D. Jett, Hamilton "Ham" Johnson, Mary Paxton Keeley, Nelle Kitchens, James Lipscomb, Freda Morris, Edwin Moss, Irma (Little) North, R. B. Price Jr., Frank St. Clair, Roy Sappington, Olive Scott, Harry E. Scurlock, Gary L. Smith, Queen Smith, Rowland H. Smith, R.L. Vickery, Frank Ward, H.J. "Jack" Waters Jr., Henry J. "Hank" Waters III, Berry Allen Watson, E. Massey Watson and Walter Williams.

Index

170

171